UNDERSTANDING EQUITATION

To Bee, Jack and John Doud
with my best wishes

[signature]

Pebble Beach
November 30. 1974

UNDERSTANDING EQUITATION

By Commandant Jean Saint-Fort Paillard

Drawings by Pierre Chambry

Foreword by William Steinkraus

DOUBLEDAY & COMPANY, INC.
Garden City, New York
1974

Library of Congress Cataloging in Publication Data
Paillard, Jean Saint-Fort.
Understanding equitation.
1. Horsemanship. I. Title
SF309.P24   789.'2
ISBN 0-385-08547-8
Library of Congress Catalog Card Number 73–20529
Book Design by BENTE HAMANN

Foreword

Why understand equitation? The question may seem frivolous and the answer self-evident, but it is clear that many riders have never bothered to do so. Perhaps this is due to a paradox that can be observed at any big show or clinic: the fact that some of the very best riders either don't know what they're doing or can't verbalize it at all, while some of the very worst can say everything right even though they do everything wrong. *Well then, the skeptic has a right to demand, just how important can understanding equitation be? Isn't doing the only thing that really counts?*

Of course doing is what counts; but *understanding* equitation makes *doing* it correctly immeasurably easier, even for those at the extreme ends of the spectrum who appear to have enough of either talent or brains to survive without revealing any of the other. It should be noted in passing that this tiny minority is even smaller than it seems, for within it masquerade both the shrewd thinker who prefers to "play dumb," and the person whose misconceptions obscure reasonably normal physical instincts. The "knowledgeable" bad rider usually belongs in this latter category, on closer examination, for there is no such thing as "paralysis by analysis" if the analysis is sound.

In any case, the possession of unusual though unbalanced physical or mental endowments scarcely concerns the vast majority of us, for most humans happily possess at least modest physical talents, which are susceptible to cultivation through exercise and practice, some modicum of educable intelligence, and some communication between the two. Thus we can entertain some hope of equestrian salvation if we can develop these resources within the framework of a sound understanding of what equitation is all about. And for us ordinary mortals, a sound conception of what we're trying to do, and why, and how, will go far to compensate for the various inadequacies of body, brain, and instinct that might otherwise doom us to permanent mediocrity.

Unfortunately, it is not easy to acquire this sound conception, for the relationship between horse and rider is both complex and capable of great subtlety. Thus horsemen on both sides of the Atlantic must be grateful to Jean Saint-Fort Paillard for having accepted the challenge of guiding our study of these fundamentals. He has brought to this task a profound knowledge of the traditions of classical equitation, broad experience on the level of Olympic dressage as both competitor and coach, a logical and inquisitive mind, and above all, great sincerity, humility, and sympathy with the horse. Commandant Paillard has anatomized the base considerations of equitation as thoroughly and clearly as I have ever seen it done, and offered many new insights that my own experience has verified. I can only hope that his penetrating and highly original work receives the wide and thoughtful readership it deserves.

WILLIAM STEINKRAUS

Contents

UNDERSTANDING EQUITATION

Introduction

Among the modern major sports, where it justly figures, riding occupies a very special place. The sport of riding is literally incomparable, for the simple and obvious reason that it alone involves a living creature—the horse—which can, of course, in no way be compared to any of the various "instruments" utilized in certain other sports. This essential characteristic of riding is responsible for its *individuality*, its *unity*, and its *diversity*.

Its *diversity* because, while riding was originally practiced for centuries almost exclusively for utilitarian purposes, civilian or military, today it offers an extraordinarily varied scale of more or less sporting activities ranging from the three Olympic disciplines, which are Jumping, Three-Day Event, and Dressage, to cross-country hacking and ordinary pleasure riding, and including such sports as racing, polo, and hunting, as well as many others.

Its *unity* because, despite the variety of these equestrian activities, all of them pose the same problems to the participating riders. In all cases, it is a question of acquiring the security and comfort in the saddle that enable one to obtain obedience from the horse. The means of solving these problems are in every case the same. The only difference is the degree of perfection with which they must be solved.

Its *individuality* because, in riding, it is always and in every circumstance the horse that accomplishes the performance and not the rider. It is the horse that races, jumps, executes a change of lead or a "passage." It is always the horse that is the performer and furnishes the required effort. This certainly does not mean to say that the rider plays only a secondary role in the performance. Quite the contrary, since it is always he who is responsible for its eventual success or failure. It does not even mean that the rider need not possess physical aptitudes, in some instances highly developed. But it does mean that riding is the *only* sport in which man's athletic ability is far less important than his technical and psychological equipment, in which sheer muscular power is far less important than sensitivity and intelligence.

This unique characteristic is undeniable, and the proof of it is the fact that the equestrian sports are the only ones in which men and women, no matter what their age (or almost), are able to compete on equal terms up to the most advanced level.

Some ill-informed individuals still find this strange, even to the point of using it as an argument to maintain that riding is a minor sport. They may be right if they attach more value to the physical than to the psychological element in their assessment of a sport, as they are perfectly free to do. But it doesn't really matter. What matters is the realization that, in riding, the athlete is the horse. The rider is simultaneously the teacher, instructor, trainer, teammate, and leader. Obviously, he can assume all these different roles only by physical means, since these are the only means of communication he has with the horse in order to make himself understood and obeyed.

One cannot "perform on" a horse as on a lifeless instrument. One induces the horse to perform. And this is what creates the originality, but also the difficulty, and finally the principal interest and the beauty of the equestrian art. It is also the factor that is responsible for all of the character-building and educational value of riding.

And yet one has only to observe what actually goes on in order to note that the vast majority of riders make much more use of their muscles than of their brains, much more use of their energy than of their intelligence and psychological understanding.

This is primarily due to the fact that the art of riding is widely misunderstood, even underestimated, by the very individuals who practice it most assiduously. And it is for this principal reason that, most often, they do not practice it as well as they might and, at any rate, do not draw from it the greatest possible pleasure and profit.

Even worse, there is an increasing number of people who want to learn to ride, but of whom only a very small percentage ever become really interested in the art of riding. The explanation is simple: their earliest instructors show them only the strictly physical aspect, which is often the only one they know but which is far from being the most fascinating. They are taught to ride more or less correctly, to use their hands and legs according to a method about as exciting as that of a driving school, and one fine day they become bored with promenades on horseback and jumping over small fences. It is all very pleasant and amusing for a while, but hardly thrilling. And sooner or later they abandon a sport they do not really understand because nobody has been capable of helping them to discover its real dimensions.

It is with the profound conviction that it is important and urgent to combat this state of affairs in the interest of the development and progress of the art of riding that I have written this book. In writing it, I have probably had in mind competitive riders most particularly, but not at all exclusively; for my true ambition is to invite all riders to contemplate, to think about what they are doing, and perhaps to reconsider their behavior entirely.

Indeed, the precise purpose of this book is to reconsider the problems of riding, simply but completely, starting from zero. I ask the reader to judge the ideas that follow with common sense and intelligence, putting aside, at least for the moment, any preconceived notions, however convincing and well assimilated they may be.

The "Great Masters" of equitation will not be summoned to support assertions that have not been previously justified. There will therefore be few quotations, which all too often encourage intellectual laziness by eliminating personal mental effort, which is the only really constructive kind. The well-informed reader will of course recognize throughout these pages familiar and even borrowed ideas, for I am concerned with reconsidering the art of riding, not with reinventing it entirely.

This book, then, by no means attempts to offer riders a method which, like all the others, would presumably lead them more effectively and quickly to better results. As a matter of fact, a method is no more than the exposition of more or less logical or empirical procedures to be applied within the limits of a particular program of work. Experience proves beyond a doubt that even the soundest riding method, no matter how meticulously and conscientiously it is applied, leads only to mediocre or poor results if it is practiced without a clear understanding of the problems to be solved and the means to be employed. And this is quite natural, since anything attempted without understanding is almost always certain to fail.

So it is this *understanding* of the problems and the means of solving them that must first of all be acquired and examined. And it is in search of it that I invite the reader to join me.

The effort to understand the art of riding leads to the establishment of certain concepts and principles which together form a "doctrine."

It is only in the light of a doctrine that the rider, understanding the whys and hows of what he is doing, can apply the procedures proposed by a method intelligently, and therefore more effectively.

I am fully aware that many people, unfortunately even among the leaders of the equestrian world, consider the term "doctrine" to be very pretentious indeed for a sport. But is it not simply because they, too, underestimate the art of riding?

I am also aware that some riders succeed brilliantly in an equestrian sport without ever having given a moment's thought to doctrine—or even, sometimes, to method. As a matter of fact, some riders, blessed with a God-given "instinctive intelligence" along with exceptional physical and moral aptitudes, have only had to develop them by more or less intensive practice in order to excel, though sometimes with a helping hand from destiny (that is, family or other favorable environment, a "perfect partner" of a horse, etc.). But I do not think I am overly pessimistic in regarding these individuals as the exceptions that prove the rule or, one might say, as lucky survivors. The others, much more numerous, submit to a system of introduction and instruction that, for want of being based on a simple, clear, and convincing doctrine, is lacking in the effective educational value that might lead them quite far toward the discovery and understanding of their sport. Consequently, as soon as they have acquired a seat they consider adequate, they launch into the practice of an instinctive kind of riding that eventually acquires consistent form only as a result of their personal research or of the examples and advice of horsemen who, for better or for worse, they choose as models.

In this hazardous quest, many go astray and never do find the way to skilled riding. Others, more fortunate, more gifted, or more determined, come more or less close to their goal, but almost always remain far behind their potential. And needless to add, the logical and inevitable consequence is that their horses, which are more or less imperfectly schooled and utilized, remain behind their potential as well, with many of their careers abbreviated or interrupted due to the physical and psychological wear and tear resulting from faulty riding and schooling.

In short, the very nature of this special sport of equitation demands that riders know and understand what they are doing, why they are doing it, and how they ought to do it in order to obtain a clearly predetermined goal.

Understanding equitation, which is essential for getting riders off to the right start and then for guiding them along the road to progress, is also necessary, even if their sporting ambitions are modest, for discovering and fully appreciating the exceptional interest and the marvelous joys that are within their reach and that they often fail to grasp because they are not even aware of their existence.

May this book help riders to discover such interest and joys.

1. What Is Equitation?

Is it really necessary that the problems of riding, which have fascinated men for so long and continue to do so, should forever remain muddled and confused?

For example, people still speak of the "French School" and the "German School," some to oppose them and others to maintain that they have finally become identical. But if some people still know what they used to be, nobody is capable, as far as I know, of stating clearly what they are today.

Besides, all over the world people ride horses, sometimes very well, without feeling the slightest need to claim membership in one school or the other—including Frenchmen and Germans. So one ends up by believing that discussions of the subject, which so easily turn into quarrels as endless and intricate as the famous Byzantine one over the sex of the angels, have become pointless and outdated.

Isn't it time, then (and haven't we taken a long time to realize it), to reconsider these riding problems?

A philosopher once said, "It is easier to solve a problem than to pose it." Perhaps. In any case, it is certainly unreasonable to claim to have solved a problem without having first posed it well, that is to say, without having established its premises as clearly and comprehensively as possible.

In the case that concerns us, the "riding problem," the solution of which has been the subject of inconclusive argument for centuries, isn't it common sense and sound logic first to try to reach an agreement as to just what the problem is, to define it, to pose it?

What is riding, after all? If we had to define it for a totally ignorant person, such as a Martian who had just landed on earth, we would probably have to say something like this: "Riding is the act of a human being's sitting astride the back of an animal called a horse, of being carried by it, and of making it obey him with the aim of utilizing it for various practical or sporting purposes."

As a matter of fact, riding in all its forms is basically no more than the art of utilizing an animal. Since man first realized that it was possible for him to subordinate certain animals to his will, through necessity or for pleasure, there have gradually emerged a few basic truths which it might be useful to recall:

● The utilization of any animal for a specific purpose, no matter how simple, is absolutely inconceivable if the animal in question has not previously been given specialized schooling for that particular purpose.

● It naturally follows that the assurance, ease, and efficiency of the utilization of an animal by man, and therefore the quality of its performance, are completely dependent on its schooling. The greater the difficulty and complexity of the utilization, the more advanced and solid should be the schooling. Otherwise, the animal's performance would be unassured, difficult, or inefficient.

● Finally, in the case of a "utilizer" who has not himself been the trainer, the quality of his utilization of an animal is exactly dependent on the precision and efficiency with which he is capable of exploiting the means previously created by the trainer.

These few self-evident truths, which are equivalent to basic principles, are perfectly valid for all animals, without exception —for parrots and elephants, falcons and dogs, dolphins and horses.

There is still another basic truth concerning the training and utilization of animals: Due to the lack of any other means of communication, it is only by making them feel physical sensations that man can make himself understood and obeyed, a combination of sensations being necessary whenever the command is not simply elementary, and a succession of sensations whenever the execution of the command has to be controlled, corrected, or modified.

These sensations may concern any of the five senses, but most often they involve the senses of sight, hearing, and touch. In some special cases, the sense of smell and even of taste can be utilized too.

Here should be inserted a word especially for equestrians, because the above truth, which is perfectly obvious to all other animal trainers and utilizers, most often seems to escape riders. At least, they generally behave as if they were unaware of it. Since they are in direct physical contact with the horse and communicate tactile sensations to it through the use of their muscles, they are easily taken in by the utterly false illusion (which is all the more convincing to them because it seems to be verified by certain superficial effects), that they act directly on the horse's body through force, and thereby obtain a sort of mechanical response.

In reality, the force they employ in their actions, consciously or unconsciously, merely creates stronger sensations, sometimes increasingly painful ones. Without realizing it (therefore more or less ineffectively), they are simply conforming to the principle formulated almost a century ago by General Alexis L'Hotte* in the very first pages of his book *Questions Équestres:* "The basis

---

* From childhood, Alexis L'Hotte (1825–1904) had a passion for equitation. As a young cavalry officer, he was the pupil of the two most famous French riding masters of his time, François Baucher and Count Antoine d'Aure. Very much in favor of outdoor riding as it was practiced in England, and which he effectively helped to introduce in France, he became one of the greatest, if not the greatest, high-school riding masters of all time. Throughout his life, he devoted his thoughtful intelligence to the study of his art, and he left two books, which were published after his death: *Questions Équestres* (Equestrian Questions) and *Souvenirs d'un Officier de Cavalerie* (Memoirs of a Cavalry Officer), republished by Émile Hazan, Paris.

of obedience in a horse, whatever it is used for, is the same. . . .
It resides solely in the animal's instinct of self-preservation,
which makes it attempt to avoid pain by responding to the
warning of factors that may cause it and may continue to cause
it, when necessary, until obedience has been obtained. Our
means of domination have no other foundation."

Thus, in a very general sense, the principle of all schooling is
to teach an animal to respond to a precise sensation with a
specific reaction, reward and punishment always being the principal means of obtaining "understanding," and sufficient repeti-
tion being the best procedure for establishing this understanding
in a lasting way.

A schooling program may be considered successfully completed when the desired reaction to the sensation created has
become like an automatic reflex and is thus the same in every
kind of circumstance. Unconditional obedience, which should
be the result of all schooling, would then be achieved, making
possible a relaxed and reliable utilization of the animal, which is
the ultimate goal.

To conclude these general principles, one more point should
be noted:

The education of a human being may be completely separate
from the use that he will eventually make of it. For example,
in the simple case of training a manual laborer, an explanation
and a demonstration of what he has to do are provided before
he is asked to do it.

The training of an animal, on the contrary, can never be
separated from the performance it makes possible. The distinct
ideas of "training" and "performance" are intermingled in actual
practice, since the result of training is necessarily an act of performance, no matter how imperfect it may be at first, and every
act of performance is at the same time an act of training, since,
according to its quality, it either improves, reinforces, or impairs
the degree of training that has already been attained.

No animal can be trained unless it is endowed with a memory.
But an animal's memory is not selective. It therefore tends to
remember all the feelings resulting from its association with

man, without being able to distinguish between what was supposed to be "training" and what was supposed to be "performance." So it retains indiscriminately all of the "lessons" it receives, consciously or subconsciously, for better or for worse. And this is why an animal's training can never be considered definitive and thus comparable to the knowledge assimilated by the human brain.

Now another word especially for riders. Those who claim that they do not school, or who even go so far as to believe and assert that it is preferable not to school the horses they ride, are simply talking *nonsense*.

It is a pity, because there are many who feel this way, but that's how it is. The fact is, of course, that *all* riders are trainers, whether they realize it or not. In any case, it is obvious that they are able to obtain performances from the horses they ride only thanks to the schooling the horses have previously received. From this point on, there are those who ride well and for whom their horses perform well, sometimes even better and better. And then there are all the others who do not ride so well or who even ride badly, and for whom their horses perform not so well, then less and less well, and finally worse and worse.

All of them are "training" every time they ride, even though they are perhaps unconscious of the fact; some of them are successful, due to their instinctive talent, and the others practically undo the training their horses have already received.

Special Conditions of Riding
That Distinguish It from Other Sports

All the ideas we have just examined, which are valid for the training and utilization of all kinds of animals, are naturally every bit as valid in the case of equitation. While the rider should continually bear them in mind, he should also be keenly aware of the two special conditions of his particular activity, for they are truly important, and he should draw conclusions from them.

● Firstly, the rider is borne by the animal he trains and utilizes;

● Secondly, as a result of this, the rider is in close and constant physical contact with the animal.

Among all the trainers and utilizers of animals, the rider is practically the only one who has to solve the problem inherent in the first condition. It is a strictly physical kind of problem, consisting as it does of remaining on the back of a moving horse, at any gait or speed, with the maximum security and comfort. The means of solving it are therefore of a gymnastic nature. Without yet being concerned with training or utilization, it is merely a question of acquiring a certain athletic technique, which consists of establishing an appropriate basic position and then of making the movements necessary to maintain equilibrium and to absorb or lessen the shocks felt. It is a technique somewhat comparable to that of skiing, for example.

It is obviously essential to acquire a perfect mastery of this technique for two reasons:

● Firstly, because it furnishes the rider with the necessary physical and mental freedom in the saddle for training and utilizing the horse in the most favorable conditions;

● Secondly, because it is only logical and fair for the rider, who naturally wants his horse to behave and perform to the best of its ability, to take care that his physical presence on the horse's back disturbs the horse as little as possible.

Thus the double goal of the rider in striving to acquire what is called "a good seat" is, on the one hand, to be completely at ease on the horse's back, and on the other hand, for the horse to be as much at ease as possible underneath him.

The ways and means of acquiring such a seat, which do not present any very subtle or complicated problems, are discussed in chapter 15.

To summarize, let us retain from this brief study of the first special condition of equitation the fact that the rider must solve an athletic problem before he can tackle his real job of training and utilizing the horse.

True, the rider should be a good athlete, but only in order to enable him to become a good trainer and a good utilizer. His athletic ability, in the purely physical sense, even if it is of the highest order, will never automatically make him a good rider. It merely furnishes him with the essential means of becoming one. He will never become a good horseman in the finest sense of the word until he has learned to make himself understood and obeyed by the horse, on which he is thenceforth at ease and perfectly in control of himself.

And this is the reason why equitation not only differs from other sports, but is also something much more than a sport.

Now we come to the second special condition of riding. Remember, it resides in the unique fact that the rider is in close and constant physical contact with the animal he wishes to train and utilize.

It is therefore important to determine how this changes his problem in comparison with that of other trainers and utilizers, and what are the advantages or inconveniences resulting from this particular condition.

To facilitate our examination of this point by making it simpler and clearer, let us compare the rider in the saddle who schools a horse and utilizes its schooling in order to perform some specific job, with the person who does exactly the same thing but remains on foot with the horse at liberty in an enclosed space. For the sake of convenience, and because no special term designates the latter, let us call him Mr. Loyal, and incidentally pay tribute to the renowned nineteenth-century French circus trainer of that name.

Sharing the same goal (making themselves understood and obeyed by the horse), they necessarily employ similar means (making the horse feel sensations in order to obtain certain reactions; that is, obedience). We can therefore fairly compare their work and learn something from the comparison.

• Mr. Loyal tries to make the horse understand and obey him by making it feel visual and aural sensations, also very rarely tactile ones by means of the longe whip, his goal being to transmit commands to the horse solely by voice and gesture.

• The rider tries to make the horse understand and obey him by making it feel almost exclusively tactile sensations, sometimes reinforced by aural or visual ones, his goal being to eliminate the latter two in order to transmit commands to the horse solely by his aids—which are nothing more than his personal means of making the horse feel sensations.

• Mr. Loyal and the rider, like all trainers and utilizers, administer rewards and punishments in order to make themselves understood and respected. However, while Mr. Loyal can quite easily offer rewards, he does not possess very many means of punishment. He is thus practically obliged to succeed solely by means of patience and tenacity, applied with gentleness, and he is virtually immune from the temptation of anger and violence, which, in his case, would immediately produce disastrous results.

• The rider, whose horse is always within his reach, so to speak, is in a much better position than Mr. Loyal to reward and punish. Where rewards are concerned, this is a great advantage, because a caress, for example, can be absolutely immediate, that is closely associated with the act that motivates it, and thus more effective. For punishment, it is also an advantage and for the same reasons. But this advantage is accompanied by the great risk of excess in frequency, duration, or severity—even in cruelty. The rider is continually exposed to the temptation of anger and violence, which are all the more dangerous because they can obtain certain instant results.

Now let's explore the comparison even further.

• When Mr. Loyal encounters a problem, as all trainers and utilizers inevitably do, he tries to make himself better understood and to increase his authority by making the horse feel clearer and stronger sensations, that is, by using a louder, more demanding tone of voice, and by making broader and more emphatic gestures. But there is no question of his letting himself go so far as to scream and gesticulate wildly, for the simple reason that he would immediately see the harmful effect and would furthermore look quite ridiculous.

• The rider in a similar situation can and should also try to make himself better understood and obeyed by making his horse feel clearer and stronger sensations. However, in his case, they are tactile sensations, and instead of first trying to produce more distinct and precise hand or leg actions, he is dangerously tempted simply to make them stronger by using greater force, and if his muscular strength is inadequate, by reinforcing his arm muscles with different systems of levers or pulleys, or by accentuating the effect of his leg muscles with more or less painful spurs. Since the use of force and pain can also obtain certain immediate results, he is dangerously exposed to the temptation of overdoing them, with the most harmful consequences. Moreover, unlike Mr. Loyal, the rider is not protected from this temptation by fear of ridicule. On the contrary, he is to a certain extent encouraged by the vain satisfaction he gets from demonstrating his strength and energy, even when the display is tainted with brutality and ignorance and finally produces poor results.

Our comparison between these two trainers and utilizers is not yet altogether complete.

• Mr. Loyal, due to his visual and aural means of communication, has a limited range of rather rudimentary signals, each of which can most often be employed only singly. He thus cannot aspire to very complex or subtle results. When, for example, he gives the command to his horse to change its gait from a walk to a canter, he can insist on obedience, but he hasn't the means to control the performance precisely. It would be extremely difficult, if not impossible, for him to get the horse to start to canter on a particular lead. Even though it is obedient, the horse thus retains a certain degree of initiative during its performance, in precision as well as in promptness.

• The rider, due to his multiple and constant contacts with his horse, has not only an extremely wide range of tactile signals but also the possibility of making several of them felt at the same time and of using them in various combinations. He can thus aspire to much more complex and subtle results and to obedience not only in the performance of the command, but also in its precision and promptness. A start in the canter, for example, would be considered satisfactory only when performed at the selected spot, on the desired lead, with straightness, calmness, and balance. All this requires a complex command from the rider, transmitted by judiciously adjusted and co-ordinated aids. It should be added that the command can be well executed only if, at the moment it is given, the horse is physically and psychologically prepared to obey it. For the rider, every command thus has to be preceded by some form of preparation or, at least, by verifying that the preliminary conditions necessary for a satisfactory performance have been established. This is a point that Mr. Loyal does not have to consider.

Now let us sum up what can be learned from our study of the second special condition of equitation:

Mr. Loyal, standing in the center of his ring, has the advantage of enjoying complete physical and psychological freedom in accomplishing his work as a trainer-utilizer. He has another advantage in the fact that, since severe, crude, or cruel means are practically excluded in his case, he is virtually obliged to develop a technique based on skill and finesse, on intelligence and psychology, if he wishes to succeed. He also cannot avoid knowing that, among horses of equal aptitude, the quality of performance will always correspond exactly to the quality of the schooling they have been given. On the other hand, his limited means of action permit him to obtain from the horse only a performance that is rather elementary, even though it may be very beautiful.

The rider has the immense advantage over Mr. Loyal of possessing infinitely superior means of action. He can therefore aspire to obtain from his horse, in any kind of work, a performance of the finest quality and in some cases of the greatest skill. On the other hand, he has to overcome two major difficulties, one physical and the other psychological, while Mr. Loyal is completely unconcerned with the first, and almost completely unconcerned with the second.

Physically, the rider must first solve the gymnastic problem of acquiring a good seat before he can, as we have seen, be in a favorable position to command the horse and at the same time prepare it most advantageously for executing his commands.

On the psychological plane, considering that he must react instantaneously to every change of behavior in his horse, he is constantly tempted to give priority to instinctive reactions over reasoned actions. Since means of force and constraint by brutality are always at his disposal, and since his instinct always urges him to employ them, he is continually exposed to the temptation of using and abusing those means in order to obtain more rapidly a certain kind of obedience.

If he is incapable of controlling his instinct and succumbs to this temptation, he is, to put it bluntly, simply practicing a method of constraint resulting from pain or fear. It is unfortunately undeniable that such a method can be effective in this field as in many others. However, apart from the degrading effect on the person who employs such a method, it not only never permits him to obtain the best possible efforts from the creature who is its victim, but it also leads the poor creature, sooner or later, according to its capacity of resistance, to a physical and psychological breakdown.

But if, possessing sufficient pride and ambition to aspire to superior results, the rider learns to control his instincts, he will, like Mr. Loyal (although certainly with greater merit), have to try to develop a technique of training and utilization that is based on intelligence and psychology—a technique he will be able to employ with maximum effectiveness and authority due to the physical self-control he has previously acquired.

The Only Worthy Kind of Riding

From this basic analysis, free from prejudice and precon- ceived ideas, there emerges a certain conception of riding, *the only one that is worthy of encouragement and preservation.*

The riding problem has now been posed.

In order to solve it, it is evident that, starting with this conception, we must consider, formulate, and put into action the most appropriate procedures and methods for training riders as well as for training and utilizing horses.

It is also in the light of this conception that we should con- demn and reject once and for all, now that men no longer have the excuse of necessity and are supposed no longer to have the excuse of ignorance, all the practices that are in the process of dishonoring modern equitation.

We are supposed to have emerged from the eras of obscuran- tism, empiricism, and cruelty; but have we really?

During the Dark Ages, the art of equitation consisted of selecting, from an array of countless bits (surely the products of some naïve anonymous lunatic), the "right one" for each particular horse. But what about all the modern riders who seem to seek the solution to their problems solely in the choice and combination of bits and bridles that are just as naïve and sometimes just as lunatic?

Certain Roman horsemen, it is said, hung from their horses' forelegs little wooden rollers which struck their cannons at every step, and they thus obtained a sort of "passage." But what about all the modern dressage riders who hit their horses' legs with whips and sticks in order to obtain what they call a "piaffe"?

As to cruelty, whoever would dare assert that it has been ban- ished from modern equitation? Aside from the torment so many riders continue to make their horses suffer on the pretext that they are schooling them, don't we know and see that violence and brutality are, unfortunately, still too widely practiced? And isn't it shocking that some of the culprits are famous riders who are able to continue with impunity to belong to what should be the elite of the equestrian world?

Isn't it deplorable that while some horsemen continue to glory in "tradition," the "educational value of equitation," and "the cavalry spirit," others continue to quarrel stubbornly over so-called "great principles" of one "school" or another?

Isn't it time for us to get rid of prejudice and preconceived ideas, and to reject a lot of erroneous beliefs and practices that are no longer really worthy of educated, civilized people such as we are supposed to have become?

Isn't it at last time to realize that, throughout the ages, riding has afforded man a unique opportunity to satisfy his innate instinct for domination, and thereby his pride and vanity? For centuries, while he was unaware that he could also apply his intelligence to equitation (which is, incidentally, not so very ancient, and from this point of view the riding fraternity is not entitled to be so proud of its past), he yielded to his instinctive reactions and tried to improve their effectiveness merely by experience and observation, without regard to reason and theory.

Shouldn't we admit, since we need only observe ourselves or others to become convinced of it, that the injudicious utilization of insufficiently or poorly schooled horses tends to encourage and develop a rider's instinctive actions, which, as we have already stressed, are not the best ones and are even usually harmful?

Shouldn't we also become aware of the fact that one of the most persistent errors of riders is a lack of intellectual honesty and a tendency to blame the horse for all of the difficulties they encounter, so as not to have to admit, to themselves as well as to others, that their problems most often originate in their own ignorance or incompetence?

Insufficiently governed by intelligence, which alone enables us to control and dominate our instincts, equitation has always produced, and unfortunately still produces, many too many snobs and brutes. Is this a tradition worth preserving?

For centuries, practical experience has been absolutely predominant, sometimes engendering theories that, because they were never put to the test of reason, had practically a single goal: to justify the existing practice. It is only common sense that, on the contrary, theory should precede practice, the soundness of which should then be verified by experience, which finally may reveal insufficiencies and errors.

A philosopher has said: "If one does not live according to one's beliefs, one ends up by believing in the way one lives."

I would like to propose for the meditation of the rider-reader an equestrian version of this maxim: "If you do not ride the way you believe you should, you end up by believing that you should ride the way you do."

2. Understanding the Horse

Everybody agrees that riders should be fairly well versed in hippology so that they know how a horse is built, how it lives, and how it moves. This is obviously necessary not only in order to keep the horse sound and get it in condition for its work, but also in order to avoid errors of utilization that go contrary to its nature.

But I firmly believe that for anybody whose ambition is to practice equitation of the finest quality, it is even more important to acquire a profound understanding of the horse's psychological makeup as an essential basis for the psychology that ought to govern its training and utilization.

It is hardly logical to go to all the trouble of getting a horse in the best possible physical condition and not give a thought to its mental conditioning, or if one does give it a thought, not to know how to go about it. It is as essential for the horse, as for any other athlete, to be in a favorable psychological state, if its physical potential is to be fully exploited. On the contrary, common sense demands that the greatest care be given to mental conditioning, and this requires quite a thorough preliminary study of the horse's psychology as it has been shaped by its living conditions throughout the ages.

It is distressing that this essential foundation of good horsemanship should be so neglected, often even completely absent from riding instruction, since disregarding it can have the most disastrous consequences. In the field of training as well as of utilization, it leads to misunderstanding and, as a result, to errors and faults that are at the root of many deplorable practices as well as many problems and disappointments.

Here I would like to pay homage to Maurice Hontang, who in 1954 published under the title *Psychology of the Horse** a book that is, to my knowledge, unique, and that every rider, every riding instructor at least, should read and study. I have incorporated a number of elements from it in the following analysis.

While the origin of the species, according to paleontologists, traces back to forty or sixty million years ago, the first sign of interest in the horse shown by man did not appear until the Stone Age, in the form of cave paintings in which *Equus caballus* is represented in herds. By then, the horse had acquired all the morphological characteristics we recognize today, although its type varied a great deal according to the influence of the soil, climate, and vegetation of the different regions it inhabited. But its principal evolution had been accomplished, and from then on these variations affected only its size and weight, thus its physical aspect, and consequently its aptitudes.

One day there occurred a great event in the history of man: for the first time, he attempted and succeeded in training the horse, thus permitting him to dominate and guide it. It seems that his original purpose was to train it to draw a chariot, and then, about 1000 B.C., to be ridden.

From that time on, the horse was a valuable collaborator of our ancestors and soon became indispensable to them, not only because of the great services it rendered in peace and war, but also due to its nobility and beauty and to the prestige it brought to those who best knew how to command obedience.

Very soon, the idea of selective breeding appeared, its principal criteria being endurance, speed, and beauty. Moreover, wars

* Published by Payot, Paris.

and conquests of distant regions led to the possibility of crossing different families of horses. The improvement of the breed thus continued for a long time in a very elementary and empirical fashion. In France, it was only in 1665, with the founding of the Corps des Gardes-Étalons (which later became the Administration des Haras), that horse breeding developed into a true science, based on a steadily increasing knowledge of the laws of zoology and genetics.

This is the long process, very briefly summarized, to which we owe our contemporary horse breeds. For the most part, they have certainly lost a great deal of their original resistance and stamina, but in exchange they have attained, from the point of view of the rider, an extremely high level of quality and a marvelous capacity for adaptation to the multiple sporting and recreational uses that have become their principal activities.

It should be added that while man, by selective breeding, has been able to shape the horse's physical aspect and aptitudes to a very appreciable extent, he has been able to exert very little influence on its psychological nature, partly because this was formed during the course of the immensely long period that preceded man's relatively recent intervention (three thousand years out of forty to sixty million years) and also because the modifications that might have been brought to it through domestication, breeding, and training are transmissible by heredity only slightly or not at all.

In order to understand the horse and the reasons for its behavior, we must thus go back to what it was in its wild state, and for that matter, what it continues to be in the few remaining regions of the world where it still lives in liberty.

The first essential element in the horse's personality originates in the fact that, as a herbivorous animal, it is not a hunter. Aggression and cruelty have therefore never been part of its nature.

Furthermore, the horse itself was hunted by wild beasts, as well as by man. However, if it is not disposed to attack, neither is it very well armed for defense. As dangerous as its jaws and hoofs may be, they are obviously not as effective as the antlers or horns with which other herbivorous animals are equipped to face an assailant.

The horse has thus been able to seek safety only in flight, a solution that is successful only when it has not been taken by surprise; in other words, when the danger has been perceived in time.

So, through the process of natural selection, as absolute conditions of survival, the horse developed senses of an exceptional acuity for detecting danger, along with an extraordinary aptitude for racing, characterized by agility and endurance as well as by speed—all of which were necessary if its flight was to succeed in saving its life.

Taking as a starting point these basic facts, which are the origin of the horse's inherited personality, now let us examine its physical and psychological nature.

On the physical plane, the horse has retained from its former life of freedom an essential characteristic: its extreme *sensitivity*. This is worth studying carefully, because, lacking any other means of learning and communication, it is through its senses alone that the horse establishes its relationships with the outside world, including man.

We will deliberately ignore the senses of smell and taste, which from the rider's point of view have little interest, in order to concentrate on the senses of touch, sight, and hearing.

The horse's sense of touch is generally very acute. In order to verify the fact, you need only observe how a fairly well-bred animal cannot bear the feeling of a mere fly on any part of its skin, although a fly is hardly capable of doing it any great harm. This is very important, since it is above all through its sense of touch that the rider communicates with the horse, in training as well as in utilization.

Let us add at once that if so many horses seem to be insensitive to spurs and even to the bit, it is certainly not through any lack of natural sensitivity, but as a result of this sensitivity being diminished by abuse, and of the gradual hardening and imperviousness that has resulted.

If the horse is in contact with its rider through its sense of touch, it apprehends the outside world mostly by sight and sound.

The word "apprehend" is used on purpose here, because it can mean "to fear" as well as "to perceive," and this is very appropriate in the case of the horse, since its sight and hearing (its sense of smell too) have always played a vital role in detecting danger. Perception and fear are therefore very often synonymous to the horse.

The horse's visual and aural sensitivities also happen to be very keen. They are definitely superior to ours, and this superior acuity is augmented by a much more extensive field of perception.

The position of its eyes, slightly bulging on each side of its head, leaves out of sight only a small blind area toward the rear. On the other hand, it should be noted that its binocular field of vision, that is to say the zone in which it can fix both eyes on the same object, is rather narrow (about 50 degrees), and one can assume, since binocular vision is necessary for judging distance, that the horse is not perfectly equipped to judge distances on the sides and to the rear.

As to its ears, which are independently mobile, they permit the horse to listen constantly for sounds coming from any direction.

In its remarkable physical sensitivity and its atavistic reflex of reacting to every strange or unexpected impression as to an alarm, lies the origin of another of the horse's principal psychological characteristics: its *emotional sensitivity*.

Visual or aural perceptions can easily set off a chain of instantaneous reactions that have all the outer aspects of fear, although—and the nuance is important—they are often in fact merely a reaction of alarm with the purpose of moving away from some presumed danger. A horse that is surprised by some sight or sound shies away from it, but usually does not flee. It was therefore not really afraid.

On the other hand, its reactions to tactile perceptions are different, since the sense of touch has never been an element of its self-defense. If the sensation felt is sudden and unexpected without being too strong, it normally provokes a reaction of surprise, a more or less violent start. But if it is strong enough to be painful, and especially if it persists, it can provoke fear and panic, as in the case of horses that run away under the effect of the heavy hand or painful spurs of a beginning rider nervously gripping the horse with his hands and legs.

Thus, the principal characteristic the horse has retained from its life of liberty is physical and emotional sensitivity (and also, to complete the picture, a certain herd instinct).

The sensitivities of wild horses have been retained to an extreme degree, due to the necessities of survival, whereas the horse's domestication and resulting security have tended to diminish them. They nevertheless subsist in a considerable measure, although naturally to a degree that varies with each animal. Still, the manner in which these characteristics are manifested depends above all on the manner in which man intervenes in the existence of each individual horse.

As a matter of fact, human intervention begins even before the foal is born, with the selection of its sire and dam. Thus, to take an extreme example, when, in his desire to inbreed, man overreaches his goal of improvement, he may produce horses so hypersensitive, therefore hyperemotive, that they are of little or no practical use outside of the racecourse.

Man's intervention is continuous from the day the animal is foaled, first in its education, including breaking, schooling, and training, then throughout its utilization.

Logically and ideally, the goal should be to safeguard the horse's physical sensitivity, which is an essential factor in successful training, resulting in easier and more effective utilization, but to suppress, or at least to diminish and control, its emotional sensitivity, which is a factor that produces difficulties in training as in utilization. This means trying to obtain its confidence in submission, and thereby calmness.

Now is the moment to ask quite objectively if riders do not very often proceed in reverse—that is, if they do not (of course, not always consciously) suppress the horse's emotional sensitivity only by more or less completely diminishing its physical sensitivity.

Aside from sluggish and apathetic horses (which owe their existence solely to their state of domestication, because the natural selectivity of wild life would never have permitted them to survive), haven't those that no longer react to very much been reduced to such a condition simply by the degradation of their sensitivity and their spirit?

Be that as it may, while its physical and emotional sensitivity may explain much of the horse's behavior, it is by no means sufficient to define its entire personality. So we must enlarge our understanding by studying the specific character of the horse's psyche. In the end, this will logically lead us to form an opinion as to the horse's intelligence, which is a vital question, since the rider's behavior toward the horse depends on it.

Without attempting to influence this opinion, let us now pass in review the horse's psychological faculties, examining them one by one and drawing some conclusions as we go along.

Memory

The first faculty that everybody admits the horse possesses, because it is incontestable, is a good memory. However, it should be noted that if memory is not the same as intelligence, it is nevertheless an essential auxiliary to it. Without memory, any durable association of ideas or feelings would be impossible. Instruction and schooling would therefore be inconceivable.

The horse's memory can record almost indelibly what it perceives through its senses. And this is a good time to recall that its relationships with man are established through its sensory perceptions, and almost entirely through its tactile sensations, as far as the rider is concerned.

The recording can be immediate, especially with a young, fresh memory, if it is the result of a very strong, violent, or painful sensation. It will be slower and more progressive if it is the result of weak but sufficiently and identically repeated sensations.

It should be apparent that this faculty of memory is double-edged, for one cannot expect the horse to record only the impressions that are useful and constructive from our point of view, and ignore all the others.

One might be tempted to compare the work of a trainer with that of a computer programmer, since both of them supply certain data, either to the horse's brain or to the computer. But this comparison would not be entirely exact. First, the electronic memory records only what it has been furnished in view of a specific utilization, whereas the horse's memory is also impressed by data received from the outside world or from previous or concurrent contacts it has had and continues to have with other people such as riders, grooms, and veterinarians, and of which the utilizer of the moment may or may not be aware.

Next, the programmer who realizes that he has provided his machine with incomplete or false information can simply withdraw it and replace it with other data. The rider does not have this option. Nothing can totally efface a remembrance recorded by a living memory. At the most, it can be gradually blurred, but only on condition that nothing happens to revive it.

Finally, even in the ideal case of a horse that has known only a single, perfect rider, it would still be impossible to count on the same sureness and automation from the animal's memory as that assured by an electronic memory, because the animal's memory can be more or less permanently troubled, even practically paralyzed, by fortuitous conditions. These may be either psychological, such as fear, distraction, nervousness, and anger, or physical, such as pain, fatigue, and illness.

Of course, the horse can remember all the sensations it records, whether tactile, aural, or visual (to limit them to the three senses that interest us the most).

As an example, let us consider its visual memory, which is perhaps the easiest to verify for certain. It is evidently very developed, especially as to places (its box in the stable, show rings, trails it has been ridden over, etc.), but also as to objects (certain types of obstacles, longe whips, nose twists, etc.). The most indelible visual remembrances generally originate in unpleasant or painful sensations, which is regrettable but only natural if the unpleasantness or pain was closely associated with the sight of the object that caused them. Thus, a glimpse of a broom or a pitchfork, if either has ever been used to strike, infallibly sets off a reaction that can very well seem unjustified when these objects do not represent a direct threat at the moment the horse happens to see them again, but it is none the less perfectly understandable.

On the other hand, the horse's visual memory of people is generally not very well developed. However, it must be admitted that riders do not do very much to develop it, since, during the time they absorb the horse's attention the most, they are sitting on its back, out of sight.

This leads us to the conclusion that while our human remembrance of persons is above all visual, the horse's is above all tactile. It is a well-known fact that a horse seems to recognize a rider with whom it has enjoyed a lengthy and impressive relationship as soon as he is in the saddle again, even after quite a long absence.

A certain visual memory can, however, be observed with grooms, who spend much more time around their charges whose appearance is regularly associated with important acts, especially feeding, and sometimes also with veterinarians, if they ever have to make rather frequent and impressive visits involving painful treatments.

The point to remember is that the horse's memory is a naturally very well-developed faculty which is always ready to function but which excludes any reasonable choice and deals solely with impressions of a physical nature.

All this makes the horse's memory a very delicate instrument for the rider to handle. But since there can be no question of training, consequently of utilization, without memory playing a part and being used to advantage, and since its resources are moreover very great and its constructive exploitation absolutely necessary to the horse's education and entire future, it is really essential to understand it and the way it works in order to avoid the risk of making many errors.

Attentiveness

The horse is capable of being very attentive, but like a child, pays attention only to what affects its senses. In particular, during all its waking moments it is "all eyes and ears."

But this is just what riders consider to be inattentiveness, since the horse's attention is quite naturally directed first of all toward the ouside world, while riders would prefer it to be completely directed toward them and their demands.

One of the first goals of schooling, and not the easiest to attain, is precisely to capture the horse's attention in spite of all the external elements that attract it. In order to facilitate the approach to this goal, it is generally recommended that one start working with young horses in an enclosed riding ring. Still, we should realize that this may be merely a more or less illusory solution if it consists only of lessening the outside distractions without taking advantage of the favorable conditions that have thus been artificially created in order to capture the horse's attention, now available, by means of schooling to the rider's aids.

The horse's attention is attracted to the outside world above all by sight and sound, whereas the rider attracts it almost exclusively by touch (sometimes by sound as well, since the voice can also be used as an aid).

The rider's problem is thus to profit from the calmness of the riding hall in order to demand gradually that the horse pay increasingly greater attention to the tactile sensations of the aids, so that eventually these tactile sensations will be able to prevail over the visual and aural sensations that attract the horse's attention to the outside world.

It must be added at once that the work accomplished in the riding hall in order to attain this goal is far removed from the routine kind of work with which riders are too often satisfied. The calmness and obedience thus obtained are often merely false appearances that more or less vanish as soon as the horse leaves the riding hall, especially since its faculties of perception—particularly visual and aural—will be more alert and will react even more keenly to unaccustomed sights and sounds.

Willpower

The horse's willpower is undeniable. In fact, man soon became acquainted with it in the form of opposition. Whether a horse's opposition is due to lack of understanding, to fear, or to any other cause, it is still an expression of willpower. It is also an act of willpower when the horse takes certain initiatives, sometimes most obstinately, such as trying to return to the stable.

Like any other faculty of the horse, this one should be exploited by the rider, and it merits careful consideration. In order to take advantage of the horse's willpower, the rider must first of all, needless to say, take care not to diminish or destroy it by severely repressing or even punishing its slightest manifestation.

With an untrained or only slightly trained horse, these manifestations should, on the contrary, be considered normal and, in all fairness, they should be combated when necessary only according to the means at the rider's disposal for making the horse understand and respect the rider's own will.

Consequently, what the rider must do is acquire the means of making himself understood and obeyed by seeking submission to the aids. He will then be able to make his will accepted, that is to say shared, for our goal is to obtain a true collaboration between the leader-rider and the subordinate-horse, which increases the effectiveness of both of them without reducing, or even worse, destroying, the subordinate's initiative.

This conception implies, of course, that the rider must be conscious of the responsibility he thus assumes. If, supposing that he has obtained such a collaboration, he takes it into his head to demand something impossible or merely too difficult, he will soon discover that the horse's will, which he believed subordinated to his own, can quite well act in opposition to him. Unfortunately, we often see numerous examples of this: for instance, in the case of racehorses that are at first generous in their efforts but that, having been taken advantage of, one day simply pin back their ears and say, "No!" It is also seen in jumpers that, having proven their willingness during a more or less lengthy career, start to stop when their riders demand too much of them or demand it incorrectly.

At the same time, is there any finer example of two wills striving toward the same goal than certain performances accomplished by great jumping riders, or certain finishes ridden by great jockeys?

Judgment, Choice, Imagination

Among the other psychological faculties of the horse, one might also mention, although they are much less evident, certain capacities for judgment, choice, and imagination.

Isn't it an act of judgment when some horses size up a strange rider? Isn't it proof of a certain capacity for choice when they sometimes seem to speculate as to the most appropriate means of opposition? And what about the horse that is able to untie itself and open its gate in order to steal hay from the food bin? Doesn't that show proof of imagination?

One could probe further into the horse's psychological faculties, but this brief analysis seems sufficient for the purposes and scope of this book, and I do not think I have succumbed to the kind of sentimentality that is so detrimental to objectivity by attempting to endow "our beloved creature" with imaginary or idealized qualities.

So, starting from this rational basis, it is now possible to pose the question of the horse's intelligence.

Is the Horse Intelligent?

In trying to reply as objectively as possible to this question, one must first of all realize that it is a particularly difficult one because the entire conception of animal intelligence remains clouded in mystery. The most recent scientific research has explored this field only superficially, but still sufficiently to refute the lazy solution of simply denying the existence of animal intelligence. Before entering into the heart of the subject, without any scientific pretension but simply with common sense, it might be useful to recall a few simple general principles.

First of all, we must remember that the idea of human intelligence is itself difficult to conceive clearly. Just think of the varying opinions held as to the intelligence of a particular person by those who believe they know him well! Furthermore, haven't you often noticed that somebody who shows remarkable intelligence in one field of activity or knowledge may very well behave like an utter idiot in another field?

Besides, it is hardly possible to evaluate the intelligence of others except within the limits of our own intelligence, which means subjectively. This is undoubtedly inevitable, but it calls for circumspection and scrupulousness. It is sometimes tempting, but really too easy, to qualify as unintelligent the people we do not understand, and also all those who do not understand us, whereas the truth may be that we ourselves have not been intelligent enough to understand or to make ourselves understood.

Finally, we form an opinion of a person's intelligence by what we know of him, by observing his behavior, but above all by conversation. Who would ever presume to judge the intelligence of a foreigner with whom, for lack of a common language, he was unable to communicate?

First conclusion: If the understanding between animals and human beings is difficult, even impossible in some cases, it is logical to admit that this might be due to our own inability to understand them and to make ourselves understood by them. As the great French moralist Montaigne wrote: So-called dumb animals may consider us just as dumb as we consider them.

Second conclusion: The problem of the horse's intelligence should be approached with modesty and objectivity. Above all, we should avoid the temptation to make hasty judgments which, by providing an excuse for our difficulties and failures, would perhaps be satisfying to our vanity but not very flattering to our intellectual honesty.

Finally, I would like to cite a discussion I once had with a young man who was generally considered to be extremely intelligent. At the time, he was riding the crest of a reputation fully justified by the extraordinary performances he got from his horses, which were not all so marvelous, and by the great success in equestrian competition that resulted. Endowed with exceptional natural gifts, he nevertheless practiced a very studied kind of equitation. But when I asked him what he thought about the horse's intelligence, he gave me a reply that was as peremptory as it was negative. It is true that concerning the intelligence of women, with whom he also enjoyed great success, his opinion, while less categorical, was hardly more favorable. With women as with horses (and I might add that his passion was equally as great for both), he possessed a certain natural power, which he did not, however, neglect to increase in effectiveness by means of technique that owed much more to intelligence than to instinct. Did this not lead him, by some paradoxical form of modesty, to underestimate his conquests? It is a well-known psychological phenomenon.

Be that as it may in this very special case, the fact remains that many people share his opinion, at least where horses are concerned, and we will intentionally restrict our study to them.

What are the reasons they give to justify this negative opinion? The most commonly cited argument is the "fear" with which horses so often react to causes that seem to us ridiculous, such as objects that do not represent the slightest threat or danger to them. Aside from being of interest in trying to evaluate the horse's intelligence, this reaction often complicates its training and utilization, and is therefore worthwhile studying in detail.

I put the word "fear" in quotation marks because the first question that arises is whether or not it really is fear that is involved. Moreover, the question has already been raised in connection with one of the basic psychological characteristics of the horse, its emotional sensitivity.

Aren't there some particularly sensitive and emotional people who start at the slightest surprise? One can question their nervous equilibrium or their self-control, but not their courage and certainly not their intelligence. A "start" is a brusque movement caused by a sudden sensation. It is, in fact, a form of direct neuromotor reaction—a reflex. Fear, on the other hand, results from the presence or idea of danger, real or imaginary; an association of ideas or of sensations thus intervenes between the perception and the reaction.

A horse that shies without trying to run away (as it would do if the fear of danger were associated with the sensation it perceived), has thus only "started," and this should be attributed to emotional sensitivity and not to fear.

Needless to say, this is not to claim that horses are afraid of nothing, but simply to note that the reactions of shy or "spooky" horses, sometimes set off by an aural or visual sensation we may not even have noticed, are very often no more than neuromotor reflexes, which have nothing to do with intelligence.

As to the real reactions of fear, as unjustified as they may be, is it fair to use them as intelligence tests? Many children are also fearful. They cry if a dog approaches them; they are afraid of the dark; they hide when a stranger arrives. This is merely an instinctive fear of the unknown or the unusual. However, with children we can offer reassuring explanations, which their young capacity of observation and reasoning ability can verify, and habit will do the rest.

But some parents who are nervous, poor psychologists, or simply stupid, on the pretext that their child is "silly to be afraid," resort to verbal or physical reprimands such as scoldings or even slaps. They thereby merely justify in a way the child's fear by associating its perception of danger, which is undoubtedly imaginary, with a disagreeable or painful sensation that is quite real. One doesn't need a Ph.D. in psychology in order to know that these parents are performing their job badly, and that by pretending to rid the child of its "silliness" in this way, they may traumatize it and, in the case of a particularly sensitive individual, even create a neurosis.

The psychology of children and of animals happens to have much in common—as does that of parents and riders, for that matter.

Obviously, it is impossible for riders to model their behavior on that of intelligent parents, that is to say, to explain to the horse that its fear is unjustified. How could they? On the other hand, it is unfortunately very easy for them to behave, consciously or not, like the stupid parents we have just described. What actually very often happens when a horse shows a lively reaction of fear? Its surprised rider is more or less displaced in the saddle; he grips with his legs, which sometimes results in an inopportune action of the spurs. As for his hands, even though they may not have involuntarily jabbed the horse's mouth due to the displacement of his seat, they are used brusquely, therefore painfully for the horse, in order to block its flight. It's lucky if the rider doesn't follow all this up by punishing with the whip or spurs! And lucky, too, if he doesn't immediately try to lead the horse back to the object that frightened it by using hand and leg actions that will be all the more violent if the horse's schooling is less advanced or if at least it is less capable of obedience in such a difficult situation without a struggle. Thus, to the horse's perception of danger (and it doesn't matter whether or not it was imaginary), the rider will have associated a whole series of disagreeable or painful sensations that are particularly traumatizing, physically and nervously.

Isn't it obvious that such behavior, though admittedly quite normally instinctive, is contrary to common sense and unworthy of human intelligence? How, then, should the rider behave in such a situation?

First of all, he should try to avoid or at least to limit as far as possible faulty actions of the seat, hands, or legs, which punish the horse, involuntarily perhaps, but at any rate unjustly, because fear is never cured by punishment.

Then he should use his aids in order to regain control, with an insistence strictly in proportion to the horse's degree of schooling. It is absolutely useless to try to exact obedience in so unfavorable a circumstance as that resulting from fear when one is already incapable of obtaining it in normal circumstances.

Finally, he should try to calm and reassure the horse, if necessary, by the comforting use of caresses and of his voice.

Force it to return to the cause of its fear? Why bother? In order to make the horse see that it is nothing more than this or that and consequently there is no reason to fear it? But this would be counting on a kind of reasoning ability that the horse is not presumed to possess. In order to show it that, frightened or not, it should always obey orders? Yes, perhaps, but on the absolute condition that the rider possesses sufficient means, that is to say, on condition that the horse's schooling is sufficiently advanced for it to be possible to do so without resorting to violence.

In general, it would seem preferable to try to pass in front of the same spot a little while later, using a firm seat and well-adjusted aids in order to absorb the animal's attention as much as possible and to distract it from what had been the cause of its fright. Then one may adapt one's behavior to the horse's reaction in accordance with the principles cited above.

Needless to say, this is not an attempt to cover the subject completely. That could fill an entire book, since the variety of individual cases is practically infinite.

My purpose is simply to offer an example of applied psychology and to draw attention to the fact that the rider's behavior is often not only unsuitable for diminishing or suppressing the horse's atavistic sensitivity and timidity, but sometimes is even apt to maintain and intensify them. Consequently, riders who blame their horses' fearfulness or timidity on lack of intelligence would do well to ask themselves first of all if they are using their own intelligence as they should.

Personally, I have come to the conclusion that the horse's

fears, or so-called fears, are merely manifestations of its great emotional sensitivity, and that they cannot be cited objectively as proof of the horse's lack of intelligence compared to other members of the animal kingdom.

Some people question the horse's intelligence by comparing it to that of other reputedly intelligent animals such as the dog, and then emphatically assert that the horse's is vastly inferior. But can such a comparison be made validly? Perhaps, but not easily, and only when one bears in mind that the original intelligence of a young creature is merely a faculty, as yet no more than a latent aptitude to learn and understand. Only later, if it has been cultivated, does this faculty develop, and only to the degree that it has been cultivated can it eventually become a capacity permitting the individual in question to be more or less intelligent in the absolute sense of the term.

This is certainly true of human beings. It is why one of the goals of civilization is or should be to give all children at the beginning of their lives the same possibilities of developing their native intelligence, that is to say, the same opportunity to acquire knowledge and understanding—although this would obviously never prevent some of them from being or becoming more intelligent than others. It is the eternal problem of inherited and acquired gifts.

This is just as true in the case of domesticated animals. It is obviously impossible to form an opinion as to their degree of innate intelligence solely according to their acquired intelligence, without taking into account the circumstances that have either helped or hindered development.

If we consider this point, it must be admitted that it is very difficult to compare fairly the horse's intelligence with that of the dog. While it is true that dogs generally display intelligence, the life they share with man, in the city as well as in the country, often from the very day they were born, is obviously most favorable to the development of their innate faculties.

On the other hand, many horses hardly seem intelligent and sometimes even seem quite stupid. But can this be considered valid proof of the lack of intelligence of an entire species? If we take into account the life we make them lead and the work we make them do, the contrary would be surprising! Spending almost all of their time with their heads tied to a wall or shut up in a stall, many of them are taken out only in order to be mounted by riders who are not even very sure of what they want, who too often get angry and punish them for no particular reason on the pretext of imposing their will, which they are incapable of communicating properly. Even though the horses may be well fed and groomed, they are reduced to a state of slavery, which understandably can lead to a state of stupor and apathy. Imagine a dog having to lead the same kind of life! Do you think its intelligence would emerge any better?

I hope that these ideas do not give the impression of being inspired by sentimentality or indignation. I know very well that with many horses, particularly with school horses, such treatment is not entirely avoidable, although much more could be done to better the lot of these unfortunate serfs.

At least the degree of degradation to which man has submitted too many horses should not be used as an argument to prove their lack of intelligence. Besides, it should be remembered that some riding-school horses, for example, develop in their misfortune an astonishing capacity for judgment and imagination. You have only to observe the often amusing scene when they "feel out a new customer" and, according to the degree of impunity they have thus estimated, decide either to get rid of him, or to make the least possible effort for him, or else to indulge in some fancy or other.

Experience has proven that a foal can very well behave with man like a dog if it has received since birth the same amount of time, attention, and affection. Like a dog, it is very quick to recognize its master, to answer to its name, to understand simple commands, games, and so forth. Unfortunately, such an experiment cannot last for long, because the foal soon grows into a horse, whose size, weight, and strength make it practically impossible to continue treatment as a house pet.

Nevertheless, many anecdotes of the Arab countries, of the Far West, of the old cavalry, too, tell of the amazingly intelligent behavior of horses that, bred and trained quite differently, had in common only the fact that they worked for a single master and almost constantly shared his life.

In short, it does not seem fair to form an opinion of the horse's intelligence by comparing it to that of the dog, or of any other domesticated animal whose conditions of life and whose education are in no way comparable.

Besides, who can claim that the dog in its wild state is more intelligent than the horse? Isn't that matter for reflection?

Do the detractors of the horse's intelligence put forward any other arguments? None that I know of, at least none that merit attention.

So it is now time to summarize and then to conclude.

● The horse possesses exceptionally keen senses, therefore an equivalent capacity of perception.

● It possesses an exceptionally good memory, therefore an equivalent capacity to record perceived sensations.

The rider, bearing in mind these two remarkable faculties, can thus through schooling—that is, through a methodical and rational system of education—make it get to *know* a great number of sensations and *learn*, by means of reward and punishment and by associations of sensations, to react in a determined way, that is, in effect, to *obey*.

Can he hope to make the horse *understand* him? As General Decarpentry wrote, the mental constitution of the horse "does not permit man to undertake separately teaching the meaning of a command and obtaining agreement as to its execution." For the rider, "making oneself understood and making oneself obeyed are one and the same thing."*

As a matter of fact, when a horse obeys a given command, who can say how much is due to understanding and how much

* General Albert Decarpentry, a French riding master who died in 1956, was President of the Dressage Committee of the Fédération Equestre Internationale after World War II and wrote several authoritative works including *Baucher et Son École* (Baucher and His School) and *Équitation Académique* (Academic Equitation), the first published by Lamarre, the second republished by Émile Hazan, both in Paris, and in English by J. A. Allen, London.

to an obedience reflex? In both cases, its brain is the connecting link between perception and the corresponding reaction. I know of nothing at our present stage of zoopsychological knowledge that would permit us to deny that the effective functioning of this connection is governed by certain cerebral processes that could be nothing else but understanding and consent.

There is good reason to believe this to be true, for it is evident even in the best-trained horse that obedience is never totally a reflex, totally automatic, thus totally certain, since the functioning of the brain connection can be altered or interrupted by fear, nervousness, or anger, for example. Would it not be the fear, nervousness, or anger that alter or prevent understanding and reduce or suppress consent? Such alterations of the cerebral functions certainly occur in man.

Finally, doesn't the behavior of a well-schooled, well-ridden horse present all the outward aspects of intelligence and consent? Doesn't a rider sometimes enjoy the keen and satisfying sensation of obtaining obedience to a command that is accepted because it has been understood? Aren't even the uninitiated also struck by this impression of understanding and consent when they have the chance to witness an example of fine riding? While this argument may not be scientific, it still may be as valid as the others.

Therefore the conclusion I propose is the following: The horse, a very sensitive creature, gifted with a fine memory, capable of great attentiveness, possessing a will of its own, and capable of judgment and imagination to a certain degree, possesses all the principal psychological attributes corresponding to the concept of animal intelligence. However, in the state of domesticated captivity in which it is held, it is up to man to assume the responsibility for developing its innate aptitude for intelligence.

Taking into account the gifts of each individual horse, the degree of intelligence it acquires will correspond to man's ability to help it attain it. In successful cases, this can place the horse in a very honorable position among the animals generally considered to be intelligent.

The fact that this opinion (which I am certainly not the first to express and defend) is not more widely shared is due primarily, I believe, to the fact that many riders, concentrated on satisfying their instinct of physical domination, do not even consider the question. Others, consciously or not, seem to prefer to avoid posing it, as if they seek to escape from the eventual embarrassment of having to adapt their behavior to the answer they will have to give, and even to completely re-evaluate their habits and their equestrian past.

Nevertheless, this question is essential, because the rider's behavior toward the horse he hopes to train and utilize, that is to say the equitation that he practices, logically depends entirely on the answer. To deny the horse any intelligence is to consider it a beast that can be trained and utilized only by force and more or less severe coercion through the exclusive use of procedures that are basically gymnastic. To recognize that the horse possesses the capacity of intelligence is to admit that equitation should abandon the path of empiricism and of instinct in order to follow that of common sense, reason, and psychology. In other words, it should be practiced in an intelligent manner, and in order to do so it must be understood.

3. The Rider's Means

In order to communicate his will to the horse and to obtain obedience, the rider has no other means, as we have seen, than to make it perceive almost exclusively tactile sensations, to which the horse will have learned to react in the desired way through appropriate schooling. The reaction thus obtained is called an "obedience reaction."

It is obvious, however, that in order to create sufficiently precise tactile sensations and to repeat them identically, which is necessary if the horse is to understand and recognize them, the rider must establish certain contacts with the horse in specific places that are always the same.

This principle is invariable. Only the means of putting it into practice can differ. In general, these means fall into one of two main categories.

The first encompasses practically all the forms of equitation that might be called "primitive" or "elementary," but without the slightest pejorative insinuation, for when they are skillfully practiced, they can obtain excellent results in the practical and simple utilization of the horse that is their goal.

In these forms of equitation, which have always been practiced in virtually the same way wherever their goal has been the same, the rider's actions, consequently the sensations perceived by the horse, are not constant but more or less intermittent. Cowboys, for example, do not maintain a constant leg contact, due to their long stirrups and the small size of their horses, and they ride with loose reins. They grip with their legs or tighten the reins briefly and only when necessary in order to communicate simple commands concerning changes of speed or direction.

This "elementary" form of equitation obviously possesses certain inconveniences. Even if the rider's actions are performed without brutality and with sufficient delicacy, they are inevitably rather sudden, thus unexpected by the horse. They therefore come as more or less of a surprise and can only provoke more or less brusque reactions, which, with very sensitive horses, can even be violent or disorganized. Furthermore, since they are not felt in a continuous manner, they cannot be expected to obtain much precision in the execution of the commands they communicate.

On the other hand, they offer advantages that, far from being negligible, are even of great value. During the periods between the rider's interventions, the horse has considerable freedom of action, permitting its natural quality and instinctive gifts (gaits, agility, sureness of foot, balance) to reveal themselves, to be improved by practice, and to achieve their full development. At the same time, its sensitivity is preserved intact due to the very fact that it is not exposed to the hardening that soon results from sensations inflicted too frequently or even continually.

The interest and value of these forms of equitation lie in these advantages, since the unconstrained, natural comportment of the horse underneath the rider is always the best guarantee of the maximum exploitation of its aptitudes. This is apart from consideration of the harmony and in some cases the beauty of its postures and movements.

Nevertheless, as great as their advantages may be, the inconveniences inherent in these forms of equitation become unacceptable whenever the rider requires a higher quality of obedience, adding precision and correctness to its unconditional and instantaneous character, and also whenever he needs to exercise constant control over the horse's performance.

Now we come to the forms of equitation that might be called "advanced" or "modern" (without necessarily investing these terms with any particularly partisan sense), and that have become necessary especially for the sporting and artistic equestrian disciplines that are most widely practiced today. The problem in these cases is to adopt a technique that diminishes or suppresses the inconveniences of the elementary forms of equitation, while safeguarding as far as possible their advantages.

Common sense dictates the only solution capable of eliminating the inconveniences: a behavior that permits the rider to constantly communicate his will to the horse. Since his will is expressed by sensations resulting from the actions of the aids, this obviously implies that these sensations must be constantly perceived by the horse, therefore that the rider's aids (hands and legs) must be constantly *in contact* with the relevant zones of perception.

In this way the horse constantly feels the aids, even when they are not active. The rider's actions, even if they are sudden, merely modify a previously perceived sensation and no longer come as a surprise to the horse, thus eliminating brusqueness and disorganization in the reactions they are designed to obtain. Moreover, they can be constantly modulated according to the horse's reactions, thus enabling the rider to control them and eventually to achieve precision in the horse's performance. The idea of contact is henceforth clearly established. For once (as is not always the case with equestrian terms!), it happens to correspond to the dictionary definition of "contact": the state of two bodies that touch each other.

In order to establish *contact* between the rider's hands and the horse's mouth, it is necessary and sufficient for them to touch each other through the intermediary of the reins and bit.

In order to establish *contact* between the rider's legs and the horse's body, it is necessary and sufficient for the legs to be in a position where they touch the horse's body.

It should be needless to add, although it is perhaps preferable to do so in view of certain opinions and erroneous beliefs, that the establishment of the contacts in no way implies any sort of *tension* of the reins, or any kind of *pressure* of the legs, except the minimum degree necessary for their continued maintenance.

Let us insert here one minor observation. When one speaks of contact, riders too often think only of the contact established by the hands. The contact of the legs is, however, every bit as important and for exactly the same reasons. Should not the traditional military order, "To your reins!" still used during cavalry training in France, be replaced by "To your aids!"? It would ring out just as well in a riding hall and would have the immense advantage, at the moment when the riders are asked to take command of their horses, of creating the reflex of really taking command, that is to say, of adjusting reins *and legs*, and of thus establishing the contacts—note the plural—necessary in order to command clearly and correctly.

It now remains to study the question of whether or not this manner of action based on constantly maintained contact risks destroying the advantages that, as we have seen, result from its suspension between two successive actions. We must therefore examine separately the case of the legs and that of the hands.

Contact and Action of the Legs

As concerns the legs, the problem is relatively simple. The contact the rider creates with the horse through his legs is readily accepted, since it is established by the supple intermediary of his boot leather with a relatively large and moderately sensitive surface of the horse's body. The very first few times a young horse is ridden, it may react with a quivering of the skin muscles; another may make a twitching motion of the head or a hind leg in the direction of the body area that has been touched, as if it wished to shake off this unaccustomed contact. But very soon it will pay no more attention to it, as the constancy and lightness of the sensation make it easy to become used to.

Starting from this *contact*, the action, which consists of nothing more than the progressive transformation of the contact into a pressure, will be just as readily accepted, without surprise at first, and even without instinctive reaction, or at most a reaction of defense or fear if it attains a degree of intensity capable of causing much constraint or, quite naturally, if it causes pain.

This is where schooling comes in. The purpose is for this leg action, which provokes a sensation perceived and accepted by the horse, to lead, by the association of sensations, to a "learned" reaction, which will be forward movement. The principles and means will be studied in the chapter devoted to impulsion.

If this schooling is satisfactory and if, as common sense dictates, the action is interrupted as soon as it has been obeyed by reducing the pressure to a simple touch—in other words, *contact*—the horse will feel no functional constraint in the execution of the command communicated. Furthermore, its sensitivity to the rider's legs will not risk becoming dulled, because it will not have been abused.

This technique of contacts thus removes the inconveniences of the "primitive" technique we mentioned, at the same time preserving its advantages. Its superiority is absolute.

Contact and Action of the Hands

As concerns the hands, the problem is more complicated and more delicate for several reasons. First of all, the contact of the hands is established through the intermediary of a steel object, the bit, with an extremely sensitive region, the horse's mouth. It is therefore felt much more keenly than the leg actions. The horse can become accustomed to it and then accept it without any other reaction only if the rider respects the essential conditions of lightness and absolute constancy. This is evidently much more difficult to accomplish with the hands than with the legs, because in order to ensure such a contact with the horse's mouth, the rider's hands must be completely independent from reactions to the gaits, whereas the horse's mouth is mobile in relation to its body. At rapid gaits it is simply inconceivable to ensure that the hands remain independent and fixed if the rider does not have a very fine seat.

But let's suppose that the seat problem has been solved and that the rider is capable of establishing a light and constant contact which the horse is able to accept without any other reaction. Now, the action of the hands, consisting of nothing more than increasing the tension of the reins from this original contact, will not necessarily be readily accepted by the horse, because, contrary to the action of the legs, it always provokes an immediate, instinctive reaction of opposition to the perceived sensation, and since this sensation affects the essentially mobile parts of the horse's body that are the head and neck, the result may be a movement, or at least an attempt to move, in the direction opposite to that of the rider's hand action.

According to whether the horse is more or less sensitive and irritable, and according to whether the rider's action is more or less tactfully performed, the horse's instinctive reaction will be expressed in a more or less active or passive manner.

If active, it will take the form of more or less violent and more or less exaggerated movements of the head and neck. The horse is then "fighting."

If passive, it is scarcely evident except in the form of a contraction without any apparent movement. The horse is then "resisting."

In order to show how important it is for the rider not simply to overlook these reactions but to act in such a way that the fighting does not occur and resisting does not appear again, it is necessary to be clearly aware of their very harmful consequences.

First of all, it is obvious that the obedience one can expect from the horse in such cases can only be very imperfect. If the horse fights, its eventual obedience can only be more or less irregular, abrupt, imprecise, and erratic. If it is satisfied merely to resist, it will obey only with more or less delay, laboriously and reluctantly.

Both cases are very far removed from a satisfactory quality of obedience, which implies consent, promptness, precision, and generosity. And this is not all. Fighting or resisting also inevitably leads to serious consequences of a physical, one might even say physiological, nature.

Firstly, the sometimes considerable nervous and muscular energy that the horse thus expends against its rider (also, needless to add, the energy expended by the rider against the horse) is completely wasted effort as far as the accomplishment of the desired movement or performance is concerned. It is absolutely contrary to the principles of economy and efficiency that common sense should impose on all riders during the training and utilization of their horses, as it is imposed on all trainers responsible for the preparation of athletes in any other kind of sport.

What is even more serious is the fact that the horse's fighting or resistance against the rider's hand more or less seriously interferes with the play of the animal's muscles and muscle groups, each of which, according to nature, should contribute to produce the requested movement. Consequently, the performance of the movement is impaired in a way that, being contrary to nature, is inevitably harmful to its quality.

When the horse fights in a very obvious way, tossing its head, twisting or throwing back its neck, etc., the situation is perfectly evident.

But when the horse does no more than resist, it is less apparent, although to different degrees, yet the fact is just the same. One need only reflect an instant in order to become convinced of it.

Even if the horse's attitude appears to be normal, even if it is placed in a way that seems correct, a horse that resists the hand is obliged to employ, aside from the jaw muscles, which have no direct effect on its locomotion, certain muscles of the neck, and in particular the muscles that tend to open the angle of the poll, and certain extensor muscles that normally should intervene only in order to balance the action of the flexor muscles.

Now, we know that there exists an instinctive correlation among all the horse's muscular contractions.

We also know that the movements of the head and neck are commanded by a very complex muscular system. And certain muscles, such as the very important mastoido-humeral one, also command the movements of the forehand, while others, such as the no less important trapezoid muscle, extend more or less toward the spinal column and have actions that are co-ordinated in various degrees with those of the muscles of the trunk itself, which in turn are co-ordinated with those of the muscles of the croup.

Finally, we know that the head and neck play the role of a balancing pole, whose displacements simultaneously lead to the modification of the balance and movements of the trunk and legs.

It is thus very clear that any constriction affecting the natural play of the neck muscles, as is the case when the horse fights against or resists the rider's hand, necessarily leads to a corresponding constriction in the play of the horse's equilibrium and of its locomotive mechanism.

• *Concerning equilibrium,* isn't it sufficiently obvious that the constant "resistance contraction" of the extensor muscles of the neck, aside from the fact that it tends to shift the horse's weight forward, constantly hampers the action of the flexor and elevator muscles, which alone can shift the horse's weight back toward the rear? The fault of horses which, when mounted, place themselves and remain "on their shoulders" generally has no other cause. We will return to this in the chapter on equilibrium.

• *Concerning locomotion,* the consequences of these resistance contractions can be infinitely varied according to their intensity, their direction, and also according to their symmetry. The fact is that almost all the muscles of the head and neck are symmetrically bilateral. If, as is almost always the case, the contractions are stronger on one side than on the other (even without any apparent change in the horse's posture), their repercussion on the muscular system is inevitably asymmetric. Irregularities of gait observed in mounted horses, especially at the trot, generally have no other cause, the best proof being that they disappear as soon as the horse is at liberty or on the longe.

The unfortunate consequences of the horse's instinctive reaction in opposing the actions of the hand are thus undeniable. It remains to be seen how it is possible to avoid them. Common sense quite obviously leads to the conclusion that it is a matter of schooling.

While schooling a horse to the legs consists of obtaining a reaction to the sensation by association with another sensation which instinctively provokes the desired reaction, schooling to the hands consists of substituting for an instinctive reaction, which is in a way a resistance reflex, a "learned" reaction of acceptance and of yielding which finally becomes an obedience reflex. This schooling is called "submission to the hand."

Very briefly, the way to accomplish it successfully consists of *making the horse discover* not only that it cannot rid itself forcibly of the unpleasant or painful sensation of the action of the hand and that, on the contrary, its forceful resistance merely makes the hand action stronger or sharper, but also that the unpleasant sensation diminishes in exact proportion to the diminishing of its own resistance and that both disappear at the same time, with the hand action being reduced to a simple sensation of contact to which the horse is already well accustomed.

In actual practice, this conception of the problem clearly dictates to the rider what he has to do:

● 1) Refuse to yield to the horse's forceful resistance to the hand and on the contrary *penalize* it by opposing an equivalent force, which should thus be no more than a force of resistance on the rider's part;

● 2) *Reward* every reduction of force that the horse employs in its reaction against the hand by the relief resulting from at least the same degree of reduction of force in the rider's resistance.

The two most serious errors to avoid are obvious:

● 1) The hand (actually the arm muscles, since the hand has no force of its own) should not exert a greater traction on the reins than that exerted by the horse itself. Doing so would tend to justify the horse's reaction of pulling even stronger against it. On the contrary, once the process has been started by the first action of the hand, the rider should leave the entire initiative of the performance to the horse and merely adapt his own behavior to the horse's.

● 2) There should not be the slightest delay in the reduction of force of the resistance of the hand, which should occur at the very moment when the counteraction of the horse begins to diminish. In order to be effective, this yielding of the hand, which should be considered a reward and employed as such, must be immediately associated with its object, that is to say with the horse's yielding. Moreover, like every reward or punishment, it should be fair, that is to say in proportion to the act that motivates it. However, in the case of a reward, one must never be afraid of being too generous, if only in order to avoid the risk of not being generous enough. Failing to yield as much as the horse has yielded amounts to failing to give all of the relief, in other words the reward, to which the horse is entitled. There is the risk of its becoming discouraged. Yielding a little more than the horse has done can, on the contrary, only encourage it—on condition that the horse is not permitted to exploit this generosity as if it were a sign of weakness or resignation and that it does not try to take advantage by resisting even more strongly. However, in such a situation, the vigilant rider need only tighten his fingers again with all the necessary firmness and without delay! It will then be the horse that punishes itself in exact proportion to its fault—and justice will be done.

In order to be thorough, and also, if not above all, to try to be as objective and honest as possible, we must mention a question that everyone avoids as if it were taboo or more or less shameful (which in fact it can be).

The truth is that the rider does not fairly combat the horse's force with his own, for the simple reason that he is quite incapable of doing so. It would be the case only if the reins were attached to a wide noseband adjusted in such a way that the horse could pull as easily as the rider can. But then all the fine theories we have been developing would be simply ridiculous, since the procedures they lead to would obviously be quite ineffective.

From the very beginnings of equitation, man has naturally been conscious of the disproportion between his own strength and that of the animal he has aspired to dominate. As always in such cases, he has resorted to the use of pain in order to shift to his advantage a struggle in which he was very unevenly matched. He has had no other choice, except to give up entirely.

Of necessity, the same principle still prevails. The force we apply to the reins is and can be effective only to the extent that it causes pain. All the various bits, hackamores, cavessons, and other devices have never had any other purpose or any other effect. As for reining devices, they do no more than modify the direction and sometimes also the force of the actions of the hand.

This is the simple and evident truth, which the most elementary intellectual honesty obliges us to recognize.

Everyone knows that all schooling is based on the use of reward and punishment. This being admitted, people generally think of reward in terms of caresses and sweets, and of punishment in the form of blows.

Schooling to the action of the hands—the "submission to the hand," if you prefer—necessarily is based on the same principles, with the difference that the punishment is administered in the form of pain coming from the hand and the bit, the reward being administered in the form of relief from this pain.

A horse is "in hand" when its rider has made it discover that all resistance on its part is instantaneously punished by pain, but that all yielding, that is to say every act of submission, is accompanied by a disappearance of this pain. It thus finds comfort in obedience, and this should be the ideal goal of all schooling, since this and this alone can lead to willingness, then to generosity, in the horse's obedience.

To the extent that he successfully accomplishes this schooling, the rider provides himself with the means of placing the horse's head and neck in the position that he wishes and of inducing the horse to assume this position without any muscular contractions other than those required in order to assume it. From this point on, always naturally, a change of *position* is necessarily accompanied by a related change of *equilibrium* and, if the rider possesses the means of setting the horse into the proper *action* with his legs, the desired *movement* is produced as if it were performed by the horse of its own volition. And we thus rediscover the basic principle of Baucher, which General Faverot de Kerbrecht, one of Baucher's best pupils, expressed as follows: Position combined with action produces movement, which is only the natural result of these two generative causes.

Then, but only then, the "technique of continual contacts" is very superior to that of the primitive forms of equitation we have described, because, in suppressing their inconveniences while safeguarding their advantages, it permits the rider to achieve a precise and constant control of his horse and to obtain a high quality of obedience—control and obedience both being essential in the modern equestrian disciplines.

In concluding this chapter, may I add the following observations?

Perhaps the reader has been shocked by the repeated use I have made of the word "pain." But he should first of all remember its true meaning: pain is merely an unpleasant sensation, not necessarily strong. Nobody can deny that the sensations created by the bit and spurs are unpleasant for the horse, even when they are not strong, and that they are certainly very painful as soon as they are intensified.

Let us try to imagine for a moment what the atmosphere in the riding hall or around a show ring would be if the horses yelped whenever they were hurt, as dogs do. Wouldn't certain jumping competitions be punctuated by howls of pain? And wouldn't certain dressage classes be punctuated by plaintive whimpers? What a nightmare!

The fact that, to their misfortune, God did not endow horses with the means of thus expressing themselves, should in no way excuse riders for not knowing (or pretending not to know) what they make their horses feel when, due to lack of proper schooling, they resort to force in order to command obedience. Shouldn't they be constantly aware of what they are doing? Let us hope that this awareness will help horsemen, who are in general certainly not brutes, to avoid behaving, without realizing it, as if they were.

Let us hope, too, that it will deprive those riders, unfortunately not so rare, who have a strong tendency toward brutality and who find in equitation an ideal occasion for satisfying it, of the excuse that they "didn't realize it." May it also deprive them of that sort of tacit encouragement resulting from the ignorant indulgence they are too often accorded, and certainly from the admiration that they often enjoy due to the successes they achieve, although their acts of torture, sometimes to the point of sadism, obviously ought to earn them the general disapproval that, curiously *except in equitation,* all acts of cruelty inspire.

4. Riding Problems

Discussions of riding problems on any level—even (or, rather, especially) on the very highest—are generally endless, often unconvincing, and almost always inconclusive. We all know this and consider it amusing, as merely an eccentricity that is by no means a monopoly of the riding fraternity. Just look at hunters, bridge players, and golfers!

On closer examination, however, the analogy between the arguments of such impassioned specialists is more apparent than real. Their principal point in common is the intense emotion of the participants. But the discussions of hunters and bridge players, for example, can draw upon an infinite variety of particular cases which furnish an inexhaustible supply of material for commentaries based on ifs and buts. They seldom degenerate into quarrels over general ideas or basic principles.

It is not the same with horsemen. Their discussions, which also most often start with very concrete particular cases, easily turn into doctrinal disputes. They bring to mind the debates of politicians, at least of certain politicians, for both have in common the fact that their efforts to understand and to convince each other are obstructed by the imprecision or the inappropriateness of the vocabulary they employ.

As a matter of fact, aren't such words as *impulsion, equilibrium, lightness* just as prone to misunderstanding, relatively speaking, as *liberty, socialism, democracy?*

At least, thank heavens, equitation poses problems that are simpler, more restricted, and certainly less abstract than the political kind!

If discussions of riding problems had only this one deficiency, it would be no matter for concern. What is worrisome is the amazing intellectual confusion from which the semantic difficulty springs and which it reveals. Confusion of words can only be the cause or effect of confused ideas. And confused ideas can naturally correspond or lead only to actions and practices that are just as confused.

So it is logical that any effort to rationalize and thereby to improve a practice must necessarily be preceded by an effort to clarify and simplify the idea behind it—it is even tempting to say "to bring it down to earth," for this often seems to be the real problem. An effort should thus first be applied to the language, that is to say, to the key words that express the different elements of riding problems and that are thus essential for formulating their terms. As every schoolchild has learned, we must first try to understand thoroughly the terms of a problem before we can try to solve it.

But in the riding halls, which are or should be schools, is enough care given to this first step? And in order to help their pupils solve the problems of riding, do riding instructors really make an effort to express and explain the elements of these problems clearly, so that the pupils really understand them? Certainly not!

Lacking a precise conception and a complete understanding of the goals to attain, the means to employ, and the difficulties to overcome, it is quite evident that the pupils can neither guide nor control their actions by their intelligence, and they are obliged to fall back upon instinct alone, with all the risks that this involves. And yet it is undeniable that anything performed with intelligence has every chance of being performed better, and this is true in every field, except perhaps in the fine arts.

But even when it is practiced in an artistic manner, riding can never be considered a pure fine art, and it thus cannot escape from the rule.

Certain individuals, however, can and do escape from this condition. There are always and always will be a few exceptionally gifted riders, possessing such a well-developed and well-adapted "horse sense" that it virtually amounts to an "instinctive intelligence" for riding, which can take the place of intelligence in the normal sense. This by no means implies any doubt as to the quality of their intellectual capacity, or even less any question as to its existence. It is simply a matter of noting that, as soon as they are on horseback, they do not use their intelligence, because they do not feel the need to do so, so totally confident are they in their intuition, their feeling, their riding tact, and their reflexes—all of them natural talents which, when developed by practice, are quite sufficient to guide them in their actions.

It is not surprising that when one asks these riders for advice or explanations, they usually employ a colorful vocabulary that is seldom precise or rigorous. This is only natural, since they are attempting to describe sensations they have never felt the need to analyze or understand.

And so the "equestrian language," encumbered by more or less unintelligible phrases, is too often complicated and obscure, which is unjustifiable in a sport that may be infinitely complex in practice but still remains simple in its principles. Its progress is all the more hindered because the language or terminology employed as an essential means of transmitting knowledge profoundly affects the value of any given instruction.

Like all techniques, equitation requires a vocabulary that is especially adapted to it, that expresses for active specialists as well as for beginners the ideas that are peculiar to it and consequently essential. These special words, consecrated by tradition and use, are thus the keys to understanding and knowledge. It is therefore important that their meanings should be clearly established. One of the greatest weaknesses of riding instruction, past and present, lies in the fact that some of the most important of these words are used without having been clearly defined to the listeners, and too often without having been completely understood by those who use them. Perhaps this helps to explain why the progress of the art of riding has been so slow throughout the ages and is still so fragile and uncertain.

The fact is that most of the great equestrian masters of former times, like many great champions today, can be numbered among those exceptional individuals whose success is due above all, if not exclusively, to their innate talent. The result is more or less empirical practices, rather than knowledge and work governed by intelligence. As impressive as their riding accomplishments may be, they have seldom contributed much to the progress of equitation in general, or to the quality of riding as practiced by others. This is because knowledge is transmissible but talent is not.

We have had and still have examples of marvelous performers who are very rarely masters, if the term is used to designate not only those who display superior ability but who also possess the talent for transmitting their art.

Teaching Means Convincing

General Alexis L'Hotte wrote very rightly that the transmission of the riding art is confronted with a particular obstacle: "the difficulty the instructor experiences in convincing his pupils." But how many modern riding instructors try to overcome this difficulty? And how many of them have there been in the entire history of equitation?

Hasn't riding instruction always been limited, except for very rare exceptions, to categorical statements supported by more or less effective demonstrations? This form of teaching has little chance of convincing, since a pupil who merely tries to imitate, that is to say, to repeat as exactly as possible, what he has been told to do in the manner in which he has been shown that it ought to be done, obviously does not obtain the same results as the instructor.

To convince is to induce somebody to accept the truth of one's assertions *through logic*. Consequently, it is possible to convince only by appealing to the reasoning ability of one's interlocutor or pupil.

It naturally follows that a personal conviction established only by empiricism and instinct cannot be transmitted, or at best only in the form of a "blind conviction," without depth or intelligence. This can doubtless offer protection from certain errors by keeping in mind certain "commandments," but it certainly cannot lead to a personal and profitable quest for improvement, nor can it discover and develop exceptional personalities, talents, and finally champions.

On the other hand, a well-reasoned and understood conviction can be transmitted validly and effectively, since, like an enlightened faith, it can guide those who have seen the light toward their goal of progress to the very limit of their abilities.

Naturally, the more clearly such a conviction is expressed in precise and simple terms, the more easily it can be transmitted to others. Which brings us back to the question of equestrian terminology.

The key words that express the ideas essential to a clear conception of the problems of riding are not so numerous.

The three famous words of General L'Hotte, "Calm, Forward, Straight," undoubtedly answered for him all his "Equestrian Questions." But, for ordinary mortals and also for riding as it is practiced today, it would seem necessary to add a few more.

The reader is therefore now invited to study the words expressing the basic ideas of riding in order to enable him to ride with the full knowledge of what he is doing, and also to be able to discuss riding with the full knowledge of what he is talking about.

Needless to say, there will be no place in this study for questions of schools or doctrines, for the principal reason that such discussions, aside from being completely outdated, never seem to have had any other result than hopelessly to confuse the simplest questions.

There will only be place (such at least is my intention) for common sense. For in the field of riding, only common sense, that is to say sound and simple logic, is truly convincing.

5. Calmness

Calmness in a living creature is the complete absence of nervousness, agitation, and disorder in its behavior.

The word "calmness" thus has a simple and perfectly clear general meaning which remains entirely valid when it is applied to horses in "equestrian language." However, the equestrian conception it expresses merits examination and reflection.

First of all, calmness is of value and interest (at least for the equitation that concerns us) only if it can be considered to be a quality of the horse. This is possible only when it is evident in the working behavior of a healthy, vigorous, and energetic animal and is not merely the result of a phlegmatic or lazy temperament, or of deficient health due to malady, malnutrition, fatigue, or physical or psychological wear and tear.

Having eliminated these last cases, let me stress the considerable, even primary importance of calmness in schooling and utilizing horses. Its importance is too seldom realized and too often ignored.

General L'Hotte, who placed it first among the three qualities he believed should characterize good riding, explained it in these terms: "All work undertaken on a nervous horse . . . can only be bad." Some people will perhaps think such a categorical opinion is valid only for dressage riding, with which General L'Hotte was mostly concerned. It must be admitted that in competitive riding sports a nervous horse which is ardent in its work is preferable to a calm horse which is reticent in its efforts. It is nevertheless undeniable that nervousness and the disorders it engenders can only be more or less seriously harmful to the quality of the desired performance, whatever it may be, and even more so to the consistency of its accomplishment.

The primary importance of calmness having been accepted, common sense requires us to discover the causes that can destroy or diminish it, and this will logically lead us to seek the means that can permit us to establish or to re-establish it, in view of these causes.

The causes of lack of calmness in a horse—in all living creatures, for that matter—may be of either a physical (organic or functional disorders) or a psychological nature.

In the first case, it can obviously be remedied only by therapeutic, dietetic, neurological, or other means affecting the animal's physical condition. This is the domain of veterinary science and not of the equestrian art, which is incapable of dealing with the basic physical causes and so can do no more than limit their effects.

On the other hand, in the second case, veterinary science can do no more than attenuate the symptoms observed, and it is the rider who possesses the means to deal with the basic psychological causes of a horse's nervousness.

It follows that it is necessary to establish a correct diagnosis at the first sign of disruption of calmness in a horse, because the remedy depends on the diagnosis.

As a general rule, at least as a first resort, it is up to the rider to make this diagnosis. In other words, he ought immediately to try to answer the following question: "Is the nervousness I notice in my horse due to a physical or to a psychological cause?" In order to answer correctly, he must use his powers of observation, his knowledge, his experience, and his psychological understanding. Above all, he should employ good faith and perfect intellectual honesty. This is not as easy as it sounds, considering the great temptation for a rider to blame his horse for the difficulties he encounters in its utilization and to reduce correspondingly, even to eliminate entirely, his own responsibility.

It is hardly possible in the course of a brief study to enumerate and analyze all the elements to be considered in establishing this diagnosis. Suffice to say that if the horse's nervousness has a strictly physical, pathological origin, it thus possesses a certain character of permanence and should manifest itself in almost all circumstances, or at least on the slightest pretext, although in varying degrees. This kind of nervousness certainly exists, but it is extremely rare.

What is very frequent, however, is the case of a horse that is calm in the stable, calm when being groomed, calm in hand, on the longe, and even at liberty, but is *nervous during mounted work*, and then immediately becomes calm again, sometimes in striking contrast to its previous behavior, as soon as its rider has dismounted. The diagnosis is then very clearly indicated, if not completely established: the cause of nervousness was none other than the rider, whose conduct and in the long run whose mere presence in the saddle had a perturbing effect on the horse's psyche.

It is unfortunate that many riders, through lack of reflection or good faith, stubbornly refuse to recognize this true cause and, instead of seeking to remedy it, simply try to attenuate its effects either by the systematic attempt (often unconscious and generally unavowed) to dispirit the horse by routine and constraint, or by physical means such as the privation of feed or tiring the horse (on the pretext of "warming up"), or even worse.* Doesn't common sense as well as intellectual honesty dictate quite a different procedure?

It should be admitted that when an otherwise calm horse becomes nervous during mounted work, it can only be due to one or more of the following causes, all of which concern the rider: a faulty seat, a bad use of the aids, a lack of schooling, or an inappropriate work program.

* Using tranquilizers is simply cheating on the part of the rider. It does not deserve any further comment.

• *A faulty seat* often causes a certain physical disorder in the horse, and this disorder easily engenders a certain nervousness. Most of the time, it is due to lack of suppleness in the rider and lack of steadiness in his hands and legs. The remedy is gymnastic work by the rider in order to acquire a good seat. (See chapter 15.) It is as simple as that.

• *A bad use of the aids*—abrupt, uneven, too insistent, badly adjusted, too strong or too weak—is also remedied solely by the efforts of the rider to improve his use of the aids. This progress alone will permit him to avoid provoking, to ameliorate, or to dispel the irritation and the resulting nervousness that rather sensitive horses inevitably manifest when they are badly commanded.

• *A lack of schooling* obviously can only be remedied by improving the situation. A sensitive horse cannot remain calm indefinitely when it is subjected to insistent and often painful demands to which it cannot respond properly because it has not been taught to understand them well.

• *An inappropriate work program* is often the result of misunderstanding and the failure to observe a few simple rules of equestrian psychology. The following are two of the most important:

> Starting to work at a walk and in slow gaits is much more effective in calming a "hot" horse than so-called "warming up" in fast gaits, which generally only excites it and is effective, but in a negative way, only when the horse has become tired.

> All work that is rather difficult, thus demanding an effort from the horse, should be frequently interrupted, either by periods of complete rest or by different exercises that are easier or more familiar, since a prolonged insistence on the same problem is always detrimental to calmness.

A fifth cause of nervousness in a horse should be added to these four principal ones: more widely recognized and admitted, at least by "outsiders," it is the possible nervousness of the rider himself. Nothing is more contagious than nervousness.

This is true of all living creatures, and horses are particularly vulnerable. Being well aware of the fact and remembering it at crucial moments is the best means of maintaining the self-control that is essential to any rider worthy of the name and that automatically dispels any possible nervousness on the rider's part.

The horse's nervousness is also terribly contagious to the rider. But a rider who is incapable of exercising patience, which is obviously necessary but not always sufficient (because patience is merely the absence of a fault and not a constructive quality), and of exercising it steadily and constantly with firm authority, runs the risk of becoming involved in the vicious circle of nervousness and anger which only leads to unsatisfactory or disastrous results.

It should be added that the problem of nervousness occurs most particularly with blooded horses, thus with temperaments that are more sensitive and consequently more emotional and irritable than most. It so happens that among these horses are found the best ones, which is an additional reason for paying great attention to the problem.

It should also be emphasized that, unlike the other qualities the rider should help his horse to acquire, such as impulsion and equilibrium, which can be fully developed only at the end of schooling, calmness should be fully obtained from the very beginning. From then on it should be maintained, or if necessary re-established, in order to avoid the risk of obtaining unsatisfactory results in all the other domains.

So calmness is in a way both the beginning and the end of a constructive schooling program. A necessary condition for a good beginning, it is then a permanent condition for profitable continuation. And finally it is one of the most eloquent proofs of success and consequently one of the best guarantees of quality and consistency in the horse's performance.

Now that we have defined and analyzed the problem, it is perhaps the moment to recall that, with the exception of pathological cases, the establishment of calmness, its maintenance, and if necessary its re-establishment are completely dependent on the psychological and technical skill of the rider.

This is not always a simple problem—far from it. Sometimes, particularly with a serious, long-lasting case of nerves, it can be very difficult indeed. To neglect or ignore it, however, as is so often done, is always a grave error. In sporting or artistic riding, it is the origin of many failures, half failures or, in the best of cases, of inconsistent performances. In fact, whatever form of equitation is practiced, it is at the very least a constant source of trouble or insecurity. If one wishes to reach a satisfactory level of equitation, one must therefore try to solve this problem as well as possible. And in order to do so successfully, one must first know what means should be employed.

What are these means? The question has already been answered above. Assuming that the essential preliminary conditions have been established (good seat and steadiness), these means are no more than schooling to the aids. Only the aids, correctly used from a technical point of view, applied with the necessary progression and precision *and above all with the necessary intelligence and psychological understanding*, make it possible to obtain a horse's submission to the rider in a spirit of confidence and respect. And only when this kind of submission has been obtained to a sufficient degree is it possible to establish and maintain calmness in the horse, or to re-establish it in a horse whose past experiences may have impaired its calmness.

This does not mean to say that the rider may not have to resort to certain supplementary precautions, such as ensuring that the horse's feed is neither too abundant nor too "heatening," verifying its stable care (the behavior of grooms, who should exercise gentleness and calm authority, is of considerable importance in this regard), judiciously selecting the environment in which the horse is schooled, etc. But none of these things is sufficient to obtain calmness if its basis in submission to the aids has not been previously established.

We have already stressed the need for the rider to use intelligence and psychological understanding in order to succeed in this area, which is often a delicate one, especially with highly bred horses. The rider should clearly understand that by observing the logical principles that ought to govern his behavior with skittish or fearful horses, he gradually influences the animal's psychology. Feeling itself supervised and controlled between the constantly and clearly felt contacts, that is to say between well-adjusted aids, being familiar with these actions, having learned to respect and to obey them, its attention is at least partially captured by the rider, and detracted to the same degree from the various sensations offered by the outside world. If the rider, then, knows how to express his will with proper precision and calm authority, always limiting his demands to what the horse is capable of doing, the submission he obtains will gradually engender confidence and respect, along with the physical and psychological ease resulting from willing obedience to a fair and clearly expressed command.

To summarize and conclude, we can affirm that lack of calmness is very rarely an intrinsic fault of horses, although they are generally highly sensitive creatures. Due to their sensitivity, a feeling of constraint and incomprehension leading to uneasiness, irritation, impatience, or—even worse—fear of the rider, can easily produce a state of nervousness. In fact, it often does so, especially in blood horses. Only by means of proper equitation and schooling can these causes of nervousness be entirely eliminated and can the elements of calmness—of the true kind, which excludes neither generosity nor even gaiety—be united, with all the priceless advantages that result.

Of course, a rider who starts to work with a new horse is not always personally responsible for the nervousness he may observe in its behavior and that may very well have been caused by the errors of one or several previous riders. But if he fails to make a scrupulous diagnosis of its origin, or if he makes a faulty diagnosis, and if he is then satisfied merely to try to limit or suppress the effects of the horse's nervousness without attempting to remedy its causes, he will obtain only mediocre results, no results at all, or even an aggravation of the affliction.

These few reflections on calmness are certainly not exhaustive, for in this domain, which is above all psychological, the variety of individual cases is unlimited.

I only hope that at least they have served to emphasize once more the fact that in riding, no procedure, technique, or method can be effective and therefore valid if it is not practiced with intelligence, that is to say, with common sense and psychological understanding.

6. Impulsion

The word "impulsion," which is derived from the Latin *pulsio* (thrust), has acquired various shades of meaning in other languages. In its literal sense, it is a mechanical term, designating both a force that provokes the movement of a body and the movement provoked by this force. Thus a cyclist gives impulsion to his bicycle by pedaling, and if he coasts along, his bicycle remains in movement due to the impulsion resulting from the force he previously applied.

In the figurative sense, the same word has a psychological meaning in many languages. An impulsion—or "impulse," as one would say in English—is also a force that drives one to action. We sometimes "give in to an impulse"—at our risk and peril, moreover, for according to the dictionary it is "an irresistible and sudden desire driving one to unreasoned acts." The French dictionary thoughtfully adds a warning against the danger of emotional and physical "impulsions."

Finally, there is the equestrian sense of the word, which is rather special and merits analysis. The first thing that immediately distinguishes the equestrian meaning from the others is that an impulsion (impulse) is a momentary force, physical, or psychological, of which the result is also momentary. But in equestrian language, we speak of impulsion and not of *an* impulsion. It is not a momentary thing at all, but a state or condition, a quality that, like all the others, is of value only because of its permanence, especially when it is put to the test of unfavorable incidents or circumstances.

How can this quality of impulsion be defined? According to the most usual formula, impulsion is the constant desire for forward movement. The term can be found in the writings of General L'Hotte, for whom this desire is manifested in the fact that the horse "places at our disposal its impulsive forces."

However, I do not believe that the word "desire" is very appropriate. While a human being can feel a desire without showing it and without seeking to satisfy it immediately for one reason or another, this is not the case with animals. Lacking innate reasoning ability, they cannot separate the desire they feel from the immediate and usually very active effort to satisfy it.

With horses, the desire for forward movement thus *has to* seek satisfaction, whatever the intention of the rider's will. And if the rider's will opposes the horse's desire by hindering, diminishing, or preventing forward movement, the rider finds himself quite simply facing the familiar problem of a spirited horse that is a "puller." One can then, if one wishes, speak of "natural impulsion."* One can say that the horse makes available its impulsive forces, but one cannot say that it makes them available *to its rider*. It should therefore be specified that impulsion is an attribute of a horse whose desire for forward movement is submitted to the rider's will.

But can a desire accurately be called "desire" when the individual who is presumed to feel it is so entirely dependent on another for expression? It is very doubtful.

That is why I prefer the following definition of impulsion:

* We should, however, be wary of the expression "natural impulsion." It should designate a spontaneous generosity, which is a characteristic of the best horses. But it certainly does not apply when this so-called generosity is no more than excitement, nervousness, or even fear, and is manifested by forward movement that is really forward flight.

the condition whereby a horse's propelling forces are constantly at the disposal of its rider for the immediate and generous execution of any requested movement.

It is then apparent that impulsion implies appropriate schooling and in fact can only be the result of schooling.

It is also apparent that impulsion is a psychological quality and that the horse's resulting physical behavior is simply a visible manifestation of this quality.

Impulsion is thus a state of generous availability, a constant consent to action, an energy always ready to be exerted.

Lack of impulsion is laziness or indolence. Excluding cases of ill health, its origin can probably be traced to unwillingness, reluctance, even stubbornness.

All this is strictly of a psychological, mental nature and indicates that impulsion is thus something else and much more than mere forward movement. It is expressed by the generosity and the apparent spontaneity of this movement.

Forward movement is no doubt proof of a certain degree of obedience to the rider's legs. But even when the forward movement is energetic, it proves the presence of good impulsion only if the rider obtains it instantaneously and effortlessly, and if, having obtained it, he does not need to do anything more in order to maintain it at the same degree of animation.

For impulsion, as we have just seen, is a state of generous availability. And what would be the value of availability and generosity that had to be originally solicited and then maintained with energy and vigor? They simply would not exist, or at least they would be of very poor quality indeed.

Does this sound like splitting hairs? Is it merely a theoretical argument? Not at all! A clear distinction between the two very different ideas of forward movement and impulsion logically leads to deductions that are vital to proper schooling and utilization, and consequently to equestrian instruction.

Obedience to the legs, which has to be taught to the horse since it is not instinctive, and which is no more than a physical reaction resulting from the creation of a neuromotor reflex, obviously cannot automatically lead to impulsion, which is, on the contrary, a psychological quality. They are two different problems. However, they are linked by the vital fact that the solution to the problem of impulsion depends on the manner in which the problem of obedience to the rider's legs has been solved. So let us now consider the latter.

When the rider closes his calves on the horse's sides, he makes it perceive a sensation that it should interpret as a command. Obedience to a command can be expected only if the command is understood, and any commander worthy of the name, in this case the rider, will ensure that this condition has been well established. If it hasn't, or has been only partially so, he will first take the necessary steps to complete the lesson. This having been accomplished, a worthy commander would never accept the position of having to repeat his order and to pronounce it more and more emphatically in order to be obeyed and continue to be obeyed. Can you imagine an army officer shouting over and over again, "Forward march! Forward march! Forward march!" in order to prevent his troops from slowing down or coming to a halt? It could be a movie "gag"! Well, the rider places himself in just such a ridiculous position when, stride after stride, he wears himself out by using his legs to maintain forward movement at the degree of animation he was able to obtain.

Isn't it only logical that, just as subordinates end up paying no attention to, even not hearing, a leader who shouts his head off all the time, horses end up no longer reacting to legs that are incessantly acting, and finally no longer feel them—except, of course, when they take it into their heads to revolt before they have become completely desensitized?

The recognition of these simple verities should completely change the rider's manner of using his legs in schooling and utilizing his horse, and also the manner in which riding instructors train their pupils in leg actions. It is obvious enough.

But let us suppose for the moment that the problem has been solved. The horse is obedient to the rider's legs, that is, to a precise but light action. It reacts immediately and willingly by producing a more energetic movement.

Having achieved this physical obedience to the legs, isn't it evident that the rider is quite close to obtaining at the same time the psychological condition of impulsion?

Finally, shouldn't we remove the mystery once and for all from this famous question of impulsion? Everything considered, how can impulsion be anything else but perfect obedience to the legs? After all, perfect obedience implies not only instantaneous and unconditional response, but also, more than willingness, the utmost generosity in the execution of a given command. The quality of the obedience is primarily dependent on the quality of the command that obtained it, and this is undoubedly even more true in equitation than in any other field. It remains true, of course, in regard to the more limited problem of obedience to the legs, the quality of which depends on the quality of the schooling given in order to create it, and of the equitation practiced afterward in order to utilize it.

Only, there is a catch. Horsemen widely proclaim the virtues of impulsion, but they are much more reticent about the means of obtaining perfect obedience to the legs, or, worse still, they advocate seeking this obedience by inappropriate means. It is the opposite of common sense. Often the same people who are always talking about impulsion criticize a rider for not using his legs *enough*, instead of telling him how to use them *better*. Or they tell a girl rider that she hasn't strong enough legs to ride a certain horse that is supposedly too much for her to handle, instead of pointing out the errors she would have to correct in order for her legs to have the necessary effectiveness. Or they mistake for impulsion the animation, perhaps quite brilliant, of a horse that constantly pulls on the reins in fast gaits, thereby manifesting not a "generous availability" but only a more or less laboriously controllable generosity. And there are countless other examples that could be cited.

Impulsion! Impulsion! How many errors have been committed in thy name!

One of the most common and also most serious is to drive young horses forward in rapid gaits by energetic leg actions, on the pretext of giving them impulsion, with the respect of reward when they obey and, the moment they slow down, of painful sensations caused by more or less severe hand actions they do not yet understand, or at least not very well. Another one is to "drive into the hands," on the pretext of establishing a "tension" that would amount to the famous impulsion, a horse that as yet understands well neither the leg actions nor the hand actions. As shocking as the simple truth may sometimes be, it should be apparent that such behavior, notwithstanding the clever words often used in an attempt to present it in another light, amounts to no more than "pushing and pulling at the same time." And this, with admirable theoretical unanimity, is condemned by everyone.

"Legs! Legs! Drive! Push onto the bit!" All this can certainly *force* a horse to move forward, and eventually make it obedient to the legs, thus permitting in the best of cases an effective utilization to a certain degree. But it will never give the horse impulsion, that supplementary quality of obedience composed of generosity and almost-spontaneity, thanks to which the rider, disposing of all of his horse's impulsive force, can hope to achieve maximum results.

As General Decarpentry put it so well, "Schooling is convincing and not forcing."

Impulsion, resulting from schooling, can logically be produced only by the scrupulous observation of the following rules, which are quite simply the rules of all sound schooling applied to this particular problem:

● 1) The action of the legs should be very clearly explained and perfectly understood.

This requires first giving the horse a "leg lesson." This lesson consists, remember, of forming an association between the sensation created by the pressure of the calves (which does not instinctively provoke the desired reaction of forward movement) and another sensation which *does* instinctively produce it. Applying the whip to the hindquarters immediately after the leg action is one of the most practical means of creating the latter sensation. A longe whip employed by an assistant can be even more effective in difficult cases. Clucking is sometimes sufficient in very simple ones.

When the association of the two sensations has been well established and forward movement is thereby easily obtained, the second sensation is progressively reduced, then eliminated entirely, and the "leg lesson" can be considered completed.

It is all too apparent that most riders do not apply themselves to accomplishing it thoroughly. As soon as the horse begins to obey the leg actions a little bit, they start to "improve" this still very incomplete obedience by intensifying their leg actions, making them stronger and more insistent. This is obviously the opposite of what should be done, since the goal is to obtain the maximum result with a minimum of action. By gradually diminishing the horse's sensitivity, it makes him more and more insensitive to the legs. The proper method, on the contrary, which consists of nothing more than perfecting the leg lesson, preserves this sensitivity and even develops it, making the horse light and responsive to the legs.

● 2) The action of the legs should be interrupted as soon as it has been obeyed. This is simply common sense. But, of course, if the obedience obtained is not sufficient, it must be remedied by seeking the basic cause. If it is due to insufficient understanding, the advice in the previous paragraph would apply. But if it is due to laziness, inattentiveness, or unwillingness, it then calls for a sharp correction, immediate and clear, and if necessary, energetic or even severe.

In any case, laboriously repeating an ineffective leg action should be absolutely excluded, and it can be seen that this second rule is a corollary of the first one.

● 3) Nothing, under any pretext whatsoever, should ever be allowed to interfere with the horse's obedience to the rider's command. General L'Hotte reports that François Baucher, the great French Master (1796–1873), used to repeat unceasingly to his riding pupils: "Open the door!" The hands, of course, represent the most dangerously effective barrier to the horse's efforts to obey the legs, and consequently to achieve the impulsion that could result. Doesn't simple common sense tell us that we should make the horse feel, and thus understand, that it will always find an open door in front of it when it is asked to move forward or to accelerate, and that when it starts to obey it will never risk being blocked by hands that remain closed, that do not yield enough or that yield too late?

● 4) The rider should help his horse discover that it will be rewarded for its obedience by the ease and comfort that result from it. It must be obvious that this comfort is already given by the interruption of the rider's action that inspired the horse's obedience and by the absence of any other action that might obstruct its response. But it should also result from the physical relief, from the sense of ease the rider should offer by ensuring as perfectly as possible his seat and steadiness during the entire procedure. And isn't it clear that if this sense of comfort is immediately associated with obedience in the horse's mind, it represents the finest possible reward and the strongest possible encouragement, infinitely clearer and more effective than caresses or lumps of sugar, which can never be given soon enough to form the proper association between cause and effect?

When these four governing principles of schooling and utilization are scrupulously respected, and when they are applied with the necessary tact (which is not some mysterious inborn gift but the result of concentrated attention by the rider), the logical result is that the horse obeys the action of the legs not because of physical constraint, but with full consent and total willingness.

Then and only then is the horse on the way to true impulsion, which complete confidence and absolute respect, resulting from sufficiently long and proper practice, will gradually bring to full development.

7. Equilibrium

After impulsion, the equilibrium of the horse, whatever it is being used for, is the principal factor in its performance and should be one of the rider's major concerns. Equilibrium in the equestrian sense is generally interpreted as being the attribute of a horse that always exercises perfect control over its mass (the weight of its body) and utilizes it appropriately according to the movements it performs. But if we want to study the question in depth, we must establish even more precisely the meaning of the word as applied to equitation and the exact conception the rider should have of it. In order to do so, we must first distinguish between the very different meanings of the word "equilibrium," according to whether it refers to inert bodies or, as in equitation, to living ones.

In the first case, equilibrium (from the Latin *aequus*—equal —and *libra*—balance) refers to the stable position of a body or a combination of inert bodies; there is a branch of mechanics, called static mechanics, which is concerned with the conditions of this equilibrium.

In the second case—the one that interests us—equilibrium is concerned not with static mechanics but with *physiology*. It is then defined as "the maintenance in space of normal relationships between the different parts of a body." This definition is just as valid for fish and birds as for horses and men. According to the encyclopedia, "the varying positions of the parts of the body and the compensatory reactions that ensue bring into play several sensorial systems, nervous and motor, which collaborate in order to ensure equilibrium."

The equilibrium of a living creature thus results from information transmitted to the central nervous system from the semicircular canals of the inner ear—complemented by the sensitive fibers that register the relative position of the different parts of the body, the areas that record the variations of pressure of the creature's footsteps, and also its eyesight.

The results of this information are motor responses that occur *without conscious control, except in abnormal circumstances*, and that govern the tension of the different muscular groups while ensuring the harmony and co-ordination of the gestures produced.

The physiological process which, whether they are standing still or moving, ensures living creatures of equilibrium, which is necessary to their survival, to their activity, and consequently to their possible utilization, is called "equilibration," a term that regrettably does not figure in the equestrian vocabulary.

Equilibration, which ensures the position of a body in space and governs all its movements—racing, jumping, etc.—is in fact the simple manifestation of what is commonly called a "sense of balance," a sort of unconscious instinct that all animals, man included, possess and maintain well developed through the constant use they necessarily make of it.

The first conclusion to be drawn from a study of the word "equilibrium" is that in equitation the problem of balance should not be thought of or posed in terms of static mechanics, but in terms of physiology, and more precisely in terms of neuromuscular physiology.

There are only two *possible* exceptions to this rule, which is a vitally important one since it destroys the false theories of "mechanics" to which so many riders succumb. Only two problems of equilibrium can in fact arise from the mechanical sense of the word:

- 1) How is the equilibrium of an unmounted horse established when it is *standing still?*

- 2) What is the effect of the rider's weight on the horse's equilibrium when it is *standing still?* (The study of this second case can be valid only if the horse perceives the presence of the rider by his weight alone, excluding all other sensations capable of provoking disturbing neuromuscular reactions.)

Let us study them briefly, remembering the results of the pertinent experiments made by General L'Hotte with a certain number of horses of various conformations: "When the horse's head is at a 45° angle from the vertical, and is held somewhat low rather than high, the weight supported by its shoulders exceeds the weight supported by its hindquarters by about one ninth of the horse's total weight." This weight distribution naturally ensures a perfectly stable equilibrium, as the vertical representing the center of gravity falls very slightly in front of the geometric center of the conveniently quadrangular figure formed by the four feet of the horse.

As to the effect of the rider's weight on this equilibrium, General L'Hotte states that "the horse carries about two thirds of the rider's weight on its shoulders, when the rider is holding his torso erect." Now, if we take the case of a horse weighing 900 pounds, carrying a rider weighing 150 pounds, it can be seen that the excess weight on the shoulders, which was 11 per cent of its mass for the unmounted horse, increases to about 14 per cent of the total mass for the mounted horse. The difference (about thirty pounds) is practically insignificant. So the first conclusion to be drawn from the study of the static equilibrium of a standing horse is the following:

It is completely untrue to claim that the rider's weight unbalances the horse to any considerable degree. It entails only a very slight modification of its natural equilibrium. A very slight change of posture thus permits the horse to re-establish it completely.

Now let us go further and examine the equilibrium of a moving horse.

Equilibration, as we have seen, is *completely instinctive in normal circumstances*. In order to continue our analysis without the risk of error, it may be useful to define exactly what are "normal circumstances."

"Normal" means anything that is habitual, that neither surprises, upsets, nor causes discomfort. Something that is not "natural" may very well become "normal," and it is what is natural that then becomes abnormal and remains so until it has become habitual again. For example, it is not natural for men to wear shoes, but it soon becomes normal. Then it is walking barefoot that becomes and remains abnormal until it becomes habitual through long enough practice.

Of course, the only really natural circumstance for a horse is to be at liberty. Everyone knows that any horse at liberty and left to its own devices, *whatever its conformation may be*— even if it has, for example, a huge head at the end of a long, thin neck, or if it is eight inches higher in the croup than at the withers—exercises perfect control over its mass, however sudden and even acrobatic its movements may be. Instinctively, it always balances itself without difficulty by adopting an appropriate posture or by modifying its posture according to the movement it makes. In other words, the horse has no more problems of equilibrium than has any other living creature.

Obviously, the act of carrying a rider *and of thus losing the initiative of its movements* creates quite abnormal circumstances for the horse. It is only logical that its function of equilibration is therefore more or less seriously affected. Just as logically, the ideal solution for re-establishing its natural adaptability consists of doing whatever is necessary in order to make the abnormal circumstances become normal. Monsieur de la Palice, a Frenchman who was famous for expressing self-evident truths, could not have phrased it better! It is not "natural" for the horse to carry a rider, but it can become "normal." Experience has proved this clearly enough, but reason must establish the conditions.

The bearing of a burden by a creature—any kind of creature —very soon becomes normal and *thus no longer alters its equilibrium on three conditions*:

● 1) that the burden be sufficiently in proportion to the bearer's strength for the effort involved not to be painfully tiring;

● 2) that the burden be distributed at the most functional support point or points, and

● 3) that the burden be constantly felt in the same way, that is to say, that the burden be perfectly united with the bearer.

The equilibration of pack mules or donkeys, for example, is in no way altered if their inert burden is rationally distributed and perfectly secured. Neither is the balance of skiers or mountain climbers perturbed if their knapsacks comply with the same conditions.

Mounted horses are also perfectly capable of controlling and conserving their equilibrium if their riders, *considered only as burdens*, also comply with these conditions—which amounts to no more than what is called having a good seat. In place of the obviously inappropriate techniques of loading and securing an inert burden, there must then be substituted the technique of acquiring a good seat. Besides, the latter is superior to the others because, by appropriate and synchronized movements, the rider can avert, absorb, or diminish the effects of an inert burden of the same weight and dimensions in cases of sudden or irregular changes of speed or direction, which are very frequent in riding. However, it should be stressed that this is true only if the rider is merely a passive burden—in other words, if he refrains from any action, voluntary or involuntary, that might provoke in the horse neuromuscular reactions other than those which instinctively ensure its functions of locomotion and equilibration.

Is this just a theoretical hypothesis? Not at all. The most perfect and striking demonstration I have ever seen of this actuality was provided by a cutting horse, ridden without a bit. As soon as its rider had pointed out the calf to be separated from the herd, the horse went to work with absolutely feline rapidity and agility and with an ease that eloquently proclaimed that the rider, as long as he possessed an imperturbable seat, didn't in the least prevent it from utilizing and adjusting its equilibrium as it pleased.

Less perfect, perhaps, but also very impressive, are the frequent demonstrations of experienced, well-trained horses whose riders, whether they be whippers-in, gauchos, cowboys, or even polo players, allow them complete freedom of movement, limiting their interventions to the strictest minimum.

Theory confirmed by experience thus permits us to formulate another very essential principle:

The rider *who does not intervene*, who behaves like a mere passenger, does not alter the horse's equilibrium *if he has a good seat*.

This being said, the rider is often obliged to intervene, particularly with young horses. Moreover, it must be admitted that no matter how good his seat may be, most of these young horses balance themselves underneath the rider more or less on their shoulders. It is also an undeniable fact that many horses obstinately cling to old habits of faulty equilibrium.

However, these same horses without exception would be perfectly balanced when at liberty. Even when mounted, they never display the slightest difficulty in shifting their weight as necessary in order to stop, turn around, back up, or rear, if they happen to feel like it. They thus show irrefutably that while their faculty of equilibration may sometimes fail to function effectively, it nevertheless remains intact. If they do not employ it as the rider wishes, the reason for it must be sought elsewhere than in some kind of innate incapacity, some inherent defect of conformation, or whatever. It must also be sought elsewhere than in the disequilibrium supposedly resulting from the rider's weight.

Then what can the reason be?

We have established that the function of equilibration, which is absolutely instinctive and naturally perfect, can be disrupted only by abnormal conditions. We have also established that the abnormal conditions resulting from the presence of the rider's weight and the manner in which he makes the horse carry it can, with habit and under certain conditions, very soon become normal. The act of carrying a rider may thus be excluded as a cause of trouble.

By the process of elimination, we are thus left with the conclusion that the only reason for a horse's difficulty in balancing itself must be due to the rider's *actions*.

The rider's actions, remember, can never have any other purpose or effect than to create sensations which, after a certain schooling, provoke certain reactions that, if the schooling has been successfully accomplished, are called obedience reactions.

It is quite evident that obedience with complete consent, that is, obedience to a command that has been understood and accepted, leaves the individual who obeys in full possession of its ability to execute the command it has received. It then acts as if of its own volition, and the conditions in which it acts are then perfectly normal.

But it is obviously not at all the same if the obedience, instead of being given with full consent, is more or less enforced. An individual who obeys only with reticence, even with resistance, finds itself in quite abnormal conditions, *psychological as well as physical,* and no longer disposes of its total abilities, natural or acquired, for the execution of the command it has received.

We have now come to the heart of the problem: the function of equilibration, a natural aptitude, is manifested only to the extent that it is not more or less seriously obstructed by the very abnormal conditions resulting from a poor acceptance of the aids. And this, after all, is quite comprehensible, since, as we have seen, a poor obedience to the aids is expressed by muscular contractions producing movements or posture that are quite different from the contractions, movements, and postures required in order to produce the performance demanded by the aids, not to mention the nervousness, fear, or anger that are so often provoked by such a situation and that so seriously alter the normal behavior of all living creatures.

Remember that the common case of horses "on their shoulders" is generally caused by the equally common fact that these horses have not been taught to understand the rider's hand actions. They consequently respond to any hand action by a reaction in the opposite direction, in this case forward, and the inevitable result is a more or less accentuated displacement of weight toward the forehand. Thus, this so-called "defect of balance," for which so many riders reproach their horses, is most of the time the consequence of a defect of schooling, and this defect comes from themselves.

Clearly such an analysis, which results from good sense and elementary intellectual honesty, changes entirely the nature of the problem and also, obviously, the means of solving it.

So, by starting with a correct definition, including a complete understanding of the horse's equilibrium in movement, we arrive at a major conclusion:

The horse's natural ability to control and adjust its equilibrium in accordance with its movements can only manifest itself fully, when the horse is mounted by a rider, if the horse accepts the action of the rider's aids.

It should be stressed that while the horse's submission to the rider's leg actions is primary in obtaining impulsion, in the case of equilibrium it is the horse's acceptance of the rider's hand actions, in a spirit of confidence and submission, that is most important. Without it, the horse's proper use of its head and neck, an absolutely essential balancing pole in its equilibration, is bound to be more or less detrimentally affected.

I will leave for later discussion the widespread but false belief that the horse requires "support" from the rider's hand in order to establish its equilibrium, and will deal with it when examining the notion of "support" (chapter 10).

And now to summarize: On the double condition that he has a good seat and that he knows how to make his actions accepted, the rider integrates the horse's aptitude for equilibrium with the circumstances.

Has the problem of equilibrium, then, been completely solved?

Yes, up to a certain level of equitation—that is to say, as long as the difficulties encountered do not exceed the possibilities of the animal's instinctive equilibration—which, incidentally, can and should be exercised and developed by calling on it to solve progressively more difficult and less natural problems. But in advanced equitation, either sporting or artistic, it is no longer true —at least, it *may* no longer be true.

In show jumping, for example, certain difficulties of modern jumping courses can exceed the capacities of the horse's animal instinct, except perhaps for a few phenomenal horses (and even then . . .). During the era of "non-intervention," these difficulties were called "horse traps." But now they should be considered problems for the rider, because in order to solve them it is the rider who must exercise his qualities of judgment, decision, and command, at least to control and often to correct the instinctive reactions of his horse.

In high-school dressage, the horse's instinct can hardly dictate the changes of balance required by the movements to be made, as the horse is not supposed to know what movements it will be asked to perform.

In both cases, it is therefore up to the rider to constantly control his horse's equilibrium so that he can judge its suitability for the jump or movement in question and modify it if necessary. He can evidently do so only by influencing the horse's posture through an appropriate use of the aids. Just as evidently, the more instantaneous and precise—in short, the more perfect —the obedience required, the more advanced must be the horse's schooling to the aids.

In conclusion, this examination of the horse's equilibrium through a strict process of reasoning based on a precise conception of the idea of equilibrium and of the riding problem it entails, permits us to formulate the following ideas:

If a horse does not display and utilize its natural qualities of equilibrium, the responsibility must then be assumed by the rider. Often, this means that he must improve his seat, and even more often, improve the use of his aids, so that the horse, which then enjoys "normal" working conditions, can manifest its "natural" instinct of equilibration.

In elementary and even intermediate equitation, a well-ridden horse that accepts its rider's actions without resistance or disorder is able to utilize all of its instinctive qualities of equilibrium.

In advanced equitation, a rider can modify his horse's equilibrium as he wishes only to exactly the same degree that he has been able to obtain submission; in other words, according to the quality of schooling he has given the horse.

Don't these ideas clearly indicate certain logical rules of action?

Once again, the most effective and sound rules of equitation come to light through reflection, through analyzing the exact meaning of a word in the equestrian vocabulary—in short, by acquiring a thorough understanding of the riding problem to which the word applies.

8. Engagement

The word "engagement," frequently used in modern equestrian language, has a very simple, very precise meaning. It is the fact that a horse brings its hind legs forward, more or less underneath its body.

A horse engages itself when, in accordance with the mechanics of the gait at which it moves, it advances its hind legs underneath its body, thus taking a succession of support points on the ground in order to propel itself forward by the play of that essentially locomotive system that is the hindquarters.

If the word leaves little room for misinterpretation, or even for discussion, it nevertheless furnishes ample matter for reflection.

First of all, it is interesting to note that common usage of the word "engagement" is relatively recent. In a way, it has taken the place in modern sporting equitation of the word *rassembler* (collection) used in classical equitation and since preserved only in academic equitation.

In order to avoid straying from the subject and to limit it, it should be noted that the words "collection" and "engagement" evoke ideas that may be definitely related but that are still very different.

Collection is a disposition of the horse's entire body, which, very succinctly, implies not only an advancement of the hind legs, but also a lowering of the croup and a corresponding raising of the forehand and neck, with the poll well flexed. It thus concerns a general *posture*, maintained for a long time and generating certain possibilities. As it obliges the horse to perform on restricted bases of support compatible only with rather slow gaits, it permits the rider to obtain maximum mobility in *all directions*, and also makes possible the maximum elevation of the gaits (compatible with their extension) and so may yield certain elevated high-school movements such as the "passage."

Engagement is merely an instantaneous movement of the hind legs, the value of which depends on its extent and on its energy. It can of course be observed in the gaits of collected horses, but it can just as well be achieved without the conditions of posture and equilibrium that characterize collection. To take an extreme example, a racehorse moving at full speed engages itself to the maximum, although its posture is the very opposite of that of collection.

This having been said, let us first examine the problem of engagement in its natural simplicity, that is to say, free from any intervention by the rider, for example in horses presented in hand and at a walk. Everyone knows that some horses engage themselves more than others, and it is interesting to ask why. It can only be for reasons either physical or psychological.

Each horse's physique obviously predisposes it more or less to engagement. A certain obliqueness of the croup, for instance, is more favorable than a horizontal one, and a rather short, strong back is more favorable than a long and sagging one.

But the horse's psychology is just as important, if not more so. By pronounced engagement, that is to say by "seeking its hoofprints" far ahead in order to walk with long strides, a horse expresses its animation and natural energy, whereas a languid, lazy horse advances with shorter steps, as if to avoid effort.

It must be admitted, however, that an exact analysis of these factors of engagement cannot be rigidly established, because the psychological factors, always difficult to grasp, increase or diminish the degree of engagement that would result solely from the physical factors in a proportion it is impossible to estimate but which is certainly important.

In any case, does it matter so much from the riding point of view? One can doubt it if one has made the following observation: Whatever its natural aptitude for engagement in normal gaits, every horse from its youngest age and without any preparation such as so-called "suppling gymnastics" is physically capable of engaging itself to a degree exactly appropriate to the movement that it *wants* to make, up to and including the most extreme.

Whatever its conformation, and on the sole condition that it is perfectly sound, every horse is capable of engaging itself to the maximum in order to pull back when tied up, for example, or to come to a sudden stop, to lunge forward, to rear, or simply to lie down.

In other words, the act of engagement, even very pronounced, is not only physically possible for all horses, but is also quite natural and easy for them.

The first conclusion to be drawn from this observation is that it is *absolutely ridiculous for the rider to claim that his horse does not engage itself sufficiently because it does not know how or is unable to do so; and it is consequently just as ridiculous to presume to teach a horse engagement.*

Nevertheless, the fact remains that horses, as capable as they may be, do not always, to put it mildly, engage themselves as it would be desirable for them to do. Having excluded inability and ignorance as possible causes, the reason must be found elsewhere. Let us therefore continue our analysis.

We have just noted that the horse engages its hind legs underneath its mass either to propel itself forward, upward, or even backward, or on the contrary to slow down or to stop. In each instance, the gesture of engagement is the same. This act merely creates a possibility either of propulsion or of braking.

Left to its own devices, at liberty or mounted, the horse naturally and instinctively engages in the exact measure of what it *wants* to do. It is thus, to return to certain examples already mentioned in regard to equilibrium, that the whipper-in's horse ridden with long reins on a rather steep downhill slope engages itself perfectly in order to "put on the brakes," just as the race-horse engages itself very strongly when the starting gate springs open, and the cutting horse displays an extraordinary engagement in order to be able to leap forward, to pirouette, or to come to a sudden stop to parry the unpredictable reactions of the calf it is supposed to separate from the herd.

So our second conclusion is the following: *Like equilibrium, the act of engagement is completely instinctive.* As long as it moves on its own initiative, the horse manifests its instinct for the correct degree of engagement just as perfectly as it manifests its instinct for the correct degree of equilibrium, according to the movement it performs.

An essential deduction emerges clearly: *Engagement becomes faulty, that is to say inappropriate to the movement, only when the horse, instead of acting on its own initiative, has to act according to the rider's will.*

Whence our third conclusion: *The origin of a defective engagement can only be the defective manner in which the rider's will is understood and accepted by the horse, or to put it bluntly, a bad submission to the aids due to insufficient schooling.*

As we saw with equilibrium, a horse that obeys with total consent remains in full possession of its means, and it then acts as if of its own volition, employing all its aptitudes, including that for engagement. On the other hand, enforced obedience resulting from a bad submission to the aids gravely alters the horse's behavior, since it inevitably engenders contractions and postures that are quite foreign and sometimes opposed to the muscular and articular functions required by the requested movement.

To summarize: If his actions are accepted—and this is an essential condition—the rider will find in his horse all of its natural and instinctive aptitude for engagement according to the movement to be made and the effort to be furnished.

Once again, common sense leads to the conclusion that in order to obtain the manifestation of the horse's latent aptitude for engagement, the rider has no other logical choice than to act on the factors that determine it and that have been mentioned above.

The rider's influence on the horse's physiological factors can only be of limited effect. He cannot modify the horse's natural conformation. At the most, he can attenuate certain deficiencies by appropriate muscular gymnastics.*

But remember that every horse, whatever its morphology, is capable of engagement, even to a very high degree, *when it wants to make a movement that requires it.* Its conformation and even its muscular system are then of relatively slight importance. The important things are its will and the energy with which the will is manifested.

We have now entered the domain of the psychological factors of engagement, on which the rider can and should act above all. And we can now formulate an obvious truth: *If the rider has made himself master of his horse's will and if he has its energy at his disposal, he simply does not need to worry about the problem of engagement, because it is then solved by the horse itself.*

Mastering his horse's will amounts to no more than obtaining absolute obedience to the aids.

Having his horse's energy at his disposal, means that the rider has developed its *impulsion.*

And we finally arrive at the simple, undeniable conclusion that *engagement is no more than the expression of impulsion in submission.*

Engagement, like collection, for that matter, is merely the result or the *effect* of which impulsion in submission is the *cause.*

To seek an effect without having previously established its cause is obviously illogical.

---

* Certain reining systems have been invented for this purpose. On condition (rather seldom fulfilled) that they be employed very methodically and above all very skillfully, they are supposed to have an appreciable corrective effect in the long run. I do not deny it, although I have personally never seen a convincing demonstration. Many times, however, I have observed their ineffectiveness, and very often their harmfulness, when they are ineptly utilized.

In the light of these truths based on simple common sense, many of the procedures recommended for developing a horse's engagement are seen to be quite irrational.

These procedures can be classified in two major categories:

First, there are all the movements more or less on two tracks, on a circle, or on a straight line that are traditionally (although incorrectly) referred to as "suppling exercises."

The principle, whose empiricism is really out of date, is to "teach" the horse to engage each of its hind legs more strongly in turn while crossing its right leg in front of its left leg, then the left leg in front of the right, and so on, in the hope that these gymnastics will increase the horse's engagement when it is moving on a straight line. But this is forgetting that no horse needs to learn engagement, nor can any kind of gymnastic exercise help it to do so, any more than a horse needs to be suppled in order to bend its spine a little or to walk sideways.

Does this mean to say that these gymnastic movements are useless, without value or interest? Certainly not. They can, on the contrary, be excellent and effective, but for quite different reasons. They can help to obtain and develop a better submission to the aids. Furthermore, due to the relaxation that naturally results from an improved acceptance of the rider's actions in the execution of a simple movement, they permit the horse's natural suppleness to manifest itself underneath the rider. Crossing the hind legs, and the increased engagement of one of them which results, are not at all the goals of these exercises. They are only the *effects*, the manifestation of submission to certain aids "in a relaxed state." They are a sort of test.

This is a good example, it seems to me, of the pre-eminence of thought over action, in equitation as elsewhere. How could it be conceivable for a particular exercise to be well performed, thus effective and constructive, if its performance is based on a false conception of its true goals? Doesn't the manner of *obtaining* suppleness necessarily imply the use of constraint in view of requiring a certain effort for the accomplishment of a naturally difficult movement? Inasmuch as relaxation is utterly incompatible with constraint as well as with effort, doesn't the manner of *establishing* it, even under the guise of the same exercise, depend on entirely different means?

Since the days of La Guérinière,* how many thousands of miles of "shoulder-ins" have been performed in vain by riders who have never been told this and who have not thought of it themselves! And it goes on and on. . . .

The second category of procedures often recommended for increasing engagement is based on a completely different principle: acting directly on the horse's muscular system in order to provoke an instinctive physiological reaction corresponding to the act of engagement.

These procedures involve actions of the heels or spurs more or less behind the girth, which are supposed to "draw the hind legs underneath the horse's body," as well as taps of the whip on the croup or back, unmounted schooling with a whip, etc.

Since these procedures are pseudo-scientific, I have thought it useful to consult in this regard "men of science," in this case highly qualified veterinarians. Having thus confirmed my own ideas by their scientific knowledge, I am in a position to make the following assertion:

Any external action on a muscle provokes a reaction of that muscle that can eventually extend to the entire muscular system to which it belongs. *But* this reaction will be the one expected (because it is normally instinctive) only if the action is applied to a horse that is in a receptive condition physically and psychologically, or at least in a state of relaxation. With a tense or nervous horse, there will always be some reaction, but it may be almost anything, according to the individual horse and to its physical and psychological condition at that particular moment.

Now is perhaps a good time to recall that the principal interest of engagement is to create or to increase the potential of propelling forces. Otherwise, it would be no more than a superficial posture without any real value—but not without a very

---

* François Robichon de la Guérinière, the founder of the French School of equitation, produced his famous work, *École de Cavalerie*, in 1751.

real danger, for it can also be the posture that permits a horse to stop or to resist forward movement.

In conclusion, the procedures of this second category can be considered useful, if one feels them absolutely necessary, when they are applied with much discretion and finesse to an already very well-schooled horse. As a matter of fact, they concern high-school dressage—and even then, except in the case of an exceptionally talented rider, the major risk they incur of harming the horse's impulsion is far greater than the importance of the results that one can hope to obtain from them. This warning is addressed to all those riders who are sporting, energetic, and vigorous (but perhaps not thoughtful enough), and who try to make their horses "engage themselves," when they are still insufficiently schooled to the aids, by means of powerful leg actions, often reinforced by spurs. How many jumping refusals have no other cause! And how many dressage horses contract, or, as is rightly said, "hold themselves back," for this simple reason!

Now we must summarize and conclude.

Since engagement is of value only when it is the result of impulsion expressed in submission, only the establishment of impulsion and submission can permit the rider to obtain his horse's engagement and to keep it at his disposal. When the rider has obtained a fairly good degree of impulsion as well as of submission, the horse will manifest its natural aptitude for engagement in the exact measure of the quality of its impulsion and submission. The level of difficulty offered by the form of equitation practiced determines the degree of impulsion and submission that should be achieved by schooling. Obviously, it does not need to be as great for a pleasure mount as for a jumper or a dressage horse.

In advanced equitation, sporting or artistic, the greatest and most difficult problem is how to act so that the horse's impulsion and submission are developed as much as possible without interfering with each other—that is to say, so that the constant generosity of the horse's impulsion remains available without hindering in the least its immediate and unconditional submission.

Only then can the rider successfully overcome difficulties that exceed the possibilities of the horse's animal instinct. For example, in high-school dressage the rider cannot count on his horse's instinct to furnish the pronounced engagement necessary for producing a "passage." But we are then in the domain of "collection," in which the engagement of the hind legs, as we have said, is only one of several factors.

In jumping, too, as soon as very difficult problems are encountered, the rider cannot count on his horse's instinct alone. He must therefore be able to affect his horse's engagement, to increase it whenever he feels that this is necessary. The most classic example of this situation occurs with a big vertical fence. To clear it without undue risk requires rather short approach strides and a somewhat rounded trajectory, which are possible only with a pronounced degree of engagement.

But how can the rider increase his horse's engagement at will? Simply by stimulating its *impulsion* and at the same time keeping it under control*—which obviously presupposes a high quality of obedience to the aids.

All of this is very simple in theory, but of course more difficult in practice. However, isn't it true that knowing what has to be done and believing in it is a necessary preliminary to learning to do it and succeeding in doing it?

The purpose of this study is precisely to establish such a preliminary.

---

* This is what all riders try to do, whether they realize it or not, when they "push and pull at the same time." But they can do it only badly, thus with doubtful effectiveness, to say the least, since they have not previously provided themselves with the means to do it well by a rather advanced schooling to the aids.

9. Tension

"Tension" is another word that symbolizes an important riding problem and has thus become current in equestrian language, but not without a certain danger, for though it is rather expressive, it easily lends itself to misunderstanding and therefore leads to deplorable practices.

First, let's examine its figurative meaning, which is what interests us here. An athlete is said to be "tensed up" for a performance when he is ready to exploit his physical means with all the required concentration and energy. Tension in this case thus concerns a phenomenon that is at the same time physical and psychological. It should be added immediately that the psychological factor is predominant, because it is obvious that the concentration and energy the athlete displays determine the intensity of his physical effort within his particular muscular limits.

The "tension" of an athlete (although the word is seldom employed in athletics in this way) is thus a psychomotor phenomenon, the value of which depends on a psychological factor. One might even say that "tension" in sporting activity is merely the physical expression of a psychological condition, in this case willpower, whatever its motivation may be.

The runner, immobile on the starting block, his muscles taut, waiting for the pistol shot to signal the start, is "wound up"; in other words, "tense."

The jumper preparing his take-off stride is also wound up, or tense.

It might be said that their neuromotor systems are placed "under tension" by the stimuli transmitted to them by their brains, which are thus clearly the original center of this tension.

If we now consider a horse at liberty, the process is exactly the same. Whether it is standing still or moving, the horse's neuromuscular tension is manifested under the influence of some psychological factor—high spirits, surprise, fear, desire, etc.—and its tension is an expression of this same emotion (from the Latin *emovere*—to set in movement) which inspired it.

A horse standing still in a field, its neck held high, its ears pricked, listening to a sound that causes it anxiety, is tense.

A horse that moves at a slow but vibrant and very high trot, with its tail over its croup and its nostrils dilated, even sometimes slipping in a few "passage" steps, is tense—just as tense as may be the horse that gallops headlong from one end of the pasture to the other.

But, of course, the word "tense" is used here in the same sense as above, which is by no means exclusive to the equestrian language.

To summarize, one can say that a horse at liberty is tense when its entire muscular system is actively employed in producing a movement or is completely prepared to produce it instantaneously and energetically, this tension being the physical expression of a psychological condition, the origin of which is not usually a deliberate intention (although this may be the case), but most often an instinctive, emotional reaction.

If we next examine this idea of tension in the case of a mounted horse, that is, in the case of equitation, the problem becomes a bit more complicated, because we then have to consider an association between two beings, thus two bodies, two neuromuscular systems, and *also two psychologies*.

Since the horse is always and in every hypothesis the sole performer, since the horse is the athlete that accomplishes the movement or the performance, it is only the horse's physical behavior that interests us here. Its state of tension does not differ in the least from the one that we have already described.

On the other hand, each of the two psychologies present obviously has an influence on it, and, according to whether they concur, complement, or oppose each other, the interpretation and the appreciation of this physical behavior are obviously different.

In equitation, the interest and value of the neuromuscular phenomenon that is called tension obviously depend on the psychological factor that provokes it.

For if one applies only the strictly physical meaning of the word, the yearling that in its first gallop pulls the arms off its exercise boy in order to catch up with the horse galloping ahead, under the simple effect of its herd instinct, even of a certain spirit of emulation, is obviously tense. The dressage horse that pulls like a locomotive because it is not submitted to the hand, is the same. The horse that launches into a series of capers either through high spirits or restiveness, is also the same. In short, the word "tension" has no interest and consequently should not be used in equestrian language unless it not only describes a certain physical behavior of the horse but also takes into account the psychological origin of this behavior.

In riding terms, tension expresses quite simply the horse's energetic and generous utilization of its muscular system, or the total and immediate availability of such a utilization, *but on the strict condition that this generous energy manifests itself only on the initiative of the rider and under his absolute control.*

Remember what we established when we were dealing with impulsion: "the condition whereby a horse's propelling forces are constantly at the disposal of its rider for the immediate and generous execution of any requested movement."

Impulsion, we said, is thus a psychological condition of the horse, and the physical behavior that results from it is merely its manifestation. We are then quite logically led to observe that the physical behavior of a horse working with impulsion is characterized precisely by the neuromuscular tension it displays.

Whence the essential conception that tension is simply the physical manifestation of impulsion and nothing else.

Consequently, as has already been said concerning impulsion, tension can be considered an equestrian quality only if it is a result of schooling.

A horse that sets off frankly from a standstill into a trot or a vibrant but submissive gallop shows that it was tense at the standstill. (If it sets off with hastiness and disorder, it simply shows that it was more or less excited or impatient to move.)

A racehorse that performs a generous canter without attempting to get out of hand, is tense. (If it fights to go faster, it is pulling and that is all.)

A horse at the piaffe (I mean a real piaffe, and not just pawing the ground) is tense in lightness (otherwise it would not piaffe).

If we are to believe Parrocel's engravings, which illustrated La Guérinière's book, the horses of La Guérinière and his pupils showed by their brilliance that they were tense in their gaits and in their airs, totally respectful of the bit and with almost loose reins.

And one can say, too, that the hunter that sets off gaily at a cheerful, regular trot while its rider, busy aiding the hounds, confidently lets it move along with loose reins, is also tense.

So we arrive at the conclusion, surprising only to those who have insufficiently pondered the question, that the quality of tension that ought to be sought and appreciated in a riding horse, a sporting horse, or a school horse, is in no way judged by the degree of tension of the reins, and that, as we have seen in the above examples, tension of the reins is not even necessarily an indication of it.

Herein certainly lies the danger of misunderstanding that makes the use of the word so current when its "equestrian meaning" is not well known. The best proof of this danger can be found in the French dictionary, where one reads among the figurative meanings of the verb *tendre*—"to make tense"—the following: *tendre* a horse: to push it forward so that it seeks support from the bit. One can certainly not condemn the author of this definition, because the figurative sense of a word is accepted when it has been established by general use, as is the case in this instance, regrettable though it may be.

It is, to tell the truth, extremely regrettable. The fact that this figurative sense of the verb *tendre*—"to make tense"—has become common enough to be accepted, merely illustrates the risk that riders constantly run of *accepting as an intelligent truth what is only a false interpretation of a physical sensation.*

A sensation should be accepted as expressing a true fact, however, only after it has been submitted to the test of reason. In the present case, such a project obliges us to recognize the following fact:

A rider does not push his horse forward to make it seek support from the bit. He does not "push the horse on his hand." These expressions, as traditional as they may be, have sufficiently proved their harmfulness, and they should be forever deleted from equestrian language. Why? Simply because they do not correspond to anything true, or even to anything possible.

When a horse is not "on the hand" or "on its bit," it means that the horse has not been schooled to accept and maintain "contact with the bit." This depends on its "schooling to the hand,"* which consists first of all in the acceptance of contact with the bit before attacking the real problem of "submission to the hand," which is much more advanced and should be the subject of the next stage of this special schooling. (Remember chapter 3, the section on "Contact and Action of the Hands.")

When a horse that submits to the hand assumes only a vague, halfhearted contact with the bit, it shows that the horse is lazy, sleepy, or halfhearted; in other words that it does not exert it-

* The expression "schooling to the hand," which oddly enough is not common, is employed here in analogy with the expression "schooling to the legs," which is very widely used.

self; in short, that it lacks impulsion. This can be corrected by schooling to the legs, as we have seen (chapter 6).

A horse that possesses impulsion and submits to the hand establishes and maintains with the bit the frank and supple contact that expresses simultaneously its impulsion and its submission to the hand. Such a horse can be described as "tense."

Of course, one can "push" a horse that lacks impulsion; in other words, force it to go faster. But if it fears the bit or does not accept it with sufficient confidence, it will not establish a good contact with it, because the horse can very well accelerate without stretching out its head and neck, and, as the rider's hand is obviously displaced to the same degree as the horse's head, the desired contact has no chance of being established.

Obviously, the rider can "force" the horse to establish this contact only by taking the initiative of backing his hands to tighten the reins, and this is, in fact, what he always does when he is supposedly only pushing the horse on the bit. But then, to put it bluntly, he is simply pushing and pulling at the same time. If that is what he wishes and what he does, he should at least have the honesty and courage to say so and not disguise it with false and hypocritical terms.

A rather insensitive horse can accept this manner of behavior. After a certain necessary period of hardening its mouth, it gets into the habit of pulling in the opposite direction. Then the reins are tightened, of course, and how! But speaking of "contact" or of "tension" in this instance would be employing farfetched euphemisms.

A horse of greater sensitivity and personality will seldom accept this manner of behavior. It will try to refuse the more or less painful constraint the rider inflicts on it either by an active defensive struggle, or by assuming an evasive posture of the neck. The rider may then try to "win" the war he has started, increasing the pain by using more brutal bits, or rendering the constraint more effective by using rein systems that forcefully maintain the horse's head and neck in position. And if his method succeeds (!), we are brought back to the previous case, since the horse will have more or less lost its sensitivity and abdicated its personality. Calling the result of this work "tension" would reflect either foolishness or dishonesty or both.

Conclusion: If the rider has a clear conception of tension in the equestrian sense, if he is profoundly convinced of what constitutes its only value and interest, if he has a thorough understanding of the factors that must be united in order to create and develop it, and if, finally, he possesses sufficient self-control and intellectual honesty to make his deeds match his convictions, he is well armed to resist the temptations of instinct and expedience, both of which lead to the blind use of force and brutality.

Then he will ride intelligently, and he will ride better.

10. Support

In equestrian language, the word "support" expresses another notion that is often misunderstood and that therefore establishes in the rider's mind a false idea, which inevitably leads him to indulge in erroneous practices. It is thus another good example of the importance of defining one's terminology if one wishes to ride intelligently, fully aware of what one is doing and of why one is doing it.

A support, in the true sense of the word, is "anything that serves to maintain something in equilibrium or to ensure its stability."

Among the numerous figurative meanings proposed by the French dictionary for the word *appui*, there is this one: "A sensation produced on the rider's hand by the tension the horse exerts on the reins." It is in this figurative sense that the word is employed in the equestrian language.

For La Guérinière, "Support is the feeling produced by the action of the bridle in the rider's hands, and reciprocally, the action that the rider's hands exert on the bars of the horse's mouth."

More recently, Count d'Aure* devoted a long paragraph to this word in his brief lexicon of "Terms in Use in the Practice of Equitation," at the end of his book *Cours d'Équitation.* His definition was the following: "The action of a horse which, in movement, places its mouth in contact with the bit, thereby establishing an intimate relationship between the horse's mouth and the rider's hand."

The word "support," as inappropriate as it may be for the figurative meaning it has been given, would thus originally express no more than an idea of "contact with the bit." But its use in this figurative sense set a veritable trap for riders, due to the fact that the tension the horse exerts on the reins is most often felt in a more or less downward direction. But weight also creates the sensation of a downward force. Consequently, certain riding masters (at least by reputation) who tried to describe their sensations to their pupils by verbal images rather than by analyzing these sensations in order to deduce convincing teachings from them, confused the idea of support with the idea of weight —at least verbally.

For example, d'Aure, commenting on his own definition of support, wrote: "The support is satisfactory when it always remains the same and has neither too much *lightness* nor too much *weight.* The support is *heavy* when the horse *weighs* on the hand and does not yield to its efforts."

It was only a step from this point to the point of identifying the sensation produced by tension of the reins with a sensation of weight, and many horsemen, even experts, gaily took it, without thinking of putting to the test of intelligent reasoning the so-called information drawn from solely instinctive perceptions.

This small false step, this *faux pas,* was and is the origin of a completely false theory according to which, since the horse takes "support," that is to say since it puts "weight" on the bit, it requires "support" from the rider's hand in order to seek or to

* Count Antoine d'Aure (1799–1863) was one of the last pupils of the famous Baron d'Abzac at the School of Versailles, which he directed at the age of twenty-eight until the closing of the school in 1830.

ensure its equilibrium. Because this theory was difficult to prove, and because nobody bothered anyway, it was accorded the status of a "principle," of a sort of article of faith, a "dogma," which true believers should accept without attempting to understand it.

However, today it is increasingly difficult to get people to accept ideas they do not understand, except perhaps in some religious or political fields. Are riders to be considered backward or mentally retarded? If not, why should they continue to accept ideas that no logical explanation can make believable?

Perhaps it is because riders are often short of ideas or knowledge for understanding their problems, that they have felt the need to create their own gods, most of whom have produced scriptures, veritable mines of dogma in which their faithful followers have had only to believe blindly. But dogma should not and cannot have a place in equestrian matters. And it is high time for equestrian instruction to stop being dogmatic.

Please excuse this digression, but the idea of support and the false dogma to which it has given rise provided an irresistible temptation. So that's that. Now let's get back to our subject.

The question was whether or not a horse can find an aid for maintaining itself in equilibrium, in other words a "support" (in the true sense of the word) from its rider's hand. The answer is: certainly not.

First of all, we have already established that the horse's equilibrium cannot and therefore should not be thought of in mechanical terms, but only in terms of its neuromuscular physiology. This in itself ought to explode the myth according to which "support" from the hand, a mechanical fact, could constitute an element of the horse's equilibrium.

If this argument should not be convincing enough to some people, the following question should suffice to open their eyes: How can a being ensure his equilibrium by seeking support from another being that he is carrying on his back? The very idea is as farfetched (and in the same category) as the one nobody even bothers to laugh at any more since it has been the butt of so many jokes: that the rider can "raise his horse over a fence" by pulling on the reins during the jump.

It should also be noted that if the impressions he feels on horseback can easily mislead an unreflective rider into thinking that support is a factor of equilibrium, the observation of mounted horses should lead him to avoid this error.

Isn't it quite apparent that horses that "lean" on the bit are almost always more or less "on their shoulders," whereas horses that refuse to take "support" from the bit are practically never on their shoulders, but on the contrary more or less balanced on their haunches? The simple truth is that, generally speaking, the first kind pull because they want to go faster, while the second remain more or less behind the rider's hand because they hold themselves back, which sufficiently explains the form of equilibrium each one adopts.

One more observation: Do horses that are used to being ridden with loose reins, in other words *without support,* such as Arabian or Western horses, show in the slightest way that they suffer from the lack of this so-called "support" in order to balance themselves? Certainly not; quite the contrary. I have, moreover, in analyzing the factors of equilibrium, explained at length why.

So let's conclude: "A horse that leans [according to a dictionary definition that happens to be right] is a horse that takes *too strong* a support on the bit," that *pulls,* and nothing more. One might say, if one insists on using the word, which is dangerous because ill-chosen, that it has "good support" when it is on the bit and does not pull. However, this really is a *good contact* (as Count d'Aure would have said) and nothing more.

The only connection between equilibrium and support is the following: Too strong a support is almost always a factor of disequilibrium, whereas the good contact of a horse submitted to the hand is an essential factor of equilibrium. But this was already one of the conclusions of our analysis of equilibrium.

Now let us rapidly examine another use of the word "support."

When a horse carries his head high enough, it can be said: "This horse has a good support" or "It lacks support," "It supports itself" or "It doesn't support itself." In these cases the word "support" expresses an idea that concerns only the manner in which the horse *supports* its head and neck or fails to do so.

A lazy or phlegmatic horse "doesn't carry its head" and lets it be carried more or less by its rider's hand. It leans on the hand. One might say that it uses the rider's hand as a headrest. And in this case the rider finds himself obliged to "support" part of *the weight of the horse's head,* justifiably feeling a sensation of heaviness.

Such a horse *weighs on the hand;* it supports its head on it; but it doesn't support itself on it; it doesn't pull in order to go faster—at least not necessarily—and its equilibrium is not *directly* concerned.

It was in this regard that François Baucher made a distinction between "resistances of weight" and "resistances of force," a distinction that is essential but sometimes delicate to establish, since these two kinds of resistance are perfectly able to coexist and even to complement each other in a way. The fact is that when the resistance of force is exerted downward, it creates a "sensation" of heaviness that adds to the one already caused by the resistance of weight. However, it is very important to distinguish between the two, because in order to dispel the resistances of force, the rider must obtain submission to the hand, whereas in order to suppress the resistances of weight, the rider must get the horse to "support itself." The two problems are quite different.

Let us limit our attention to the resistances of weight, which are the only ones pertinent to our subject. The *half-halt,* which is the recommended counteraction, should thus be understood and consequently performed as a measure designed to get the horse to make an effort to support its head and neck by making it understand that it cannot find a "support" in the rider's hand that would permit it to avoid this effort. The purpose of this half-halt is thus to get the horse to assume and maintain a certain posture, which is precisely a *posture of support.** Naturally, according to whether the head and neck are held more or less high, this posture corresponds to an equilibrium in which the shoulders are more or less unburdened, while the hindquarters are burdened to the same degree.

Once again, isn't it clear that the accurate understanding of a word and the idea it expresses conditions the quality of the action it inspires?

In this instance, a rider who tries to make his horse assume and maintain a certain posture by performing a half-halt will obtain *as a logical consequence* a certain modification of its equilibrium, but he will be acting very differently from the rider who thinks he has to make the same half-halt in order to intervene directly in the horse's equilibrium and, as is very ineptly stated in the official French equestrian manual, "to transfer to the hindquarters the excess weight that certain badly balanced horses carry on their shoulders."

It is true that this manual also recommends half-halts "for slowing down horses that are too high-spirited!"

It is true, too, that the term "half-halt" is an unfortunate one. On first impression, it seems to describe an action of the hands designed to get the horse to stop halfway, that is to say, to effect a very pronounced and rapid, if not brusque, deceleration. But such an action is related more to the "parade" dressage movement—at least to what many people modestly designate by this term, or more simply to the "saccade"—when it is not simply a yank.

However, as ill-chosen as may be the words "support" and "half-halt," it would still be desirable to adhere strictly to their original meanings. At least they would no longer be used to mask an unthinking kind of equitation—and a bad one.

---

* The idea that ought to be behind the performance of a half-halt might be compared to the little upward push, of varying pressure according to the circumstances but always very brief, given by a professor who pushes his finger under the chin of a pupil slumped over his desk, saying, "Sit up straight!" With a half-halt, signaled by a slight brief lifting of the reins, the rider tells his horse, "Hold yourself better! Support your neck!" And remember that for horses as for children, a head held high is a sign of alertness, thus favorable to activity, and not merely a posture of conventional "good bearing."

11. Straightness

"Straight: Applies to something that goes without deviation, without a curve, from one point to another." This is the true definition of the word. In its simplicity, it defines the shortest route from one point to another, but it can also very well be applied to a horse that rigorously follows such a route or that stops exactly on it.

At a standstill, a horse is straight when the entire length of its spine is in the vertical plane containing the straight line drawn between the point at which it stopped and the point toward which it was moving.

In movement, the definition of a straight horse cannot be as precise, due to the lateral movements of the spine required by each gait. So a horse can be considered to move straight when its hind feet exactly follow the rectilinear tracks of the forefeet, these tracks being parallel to the straight line the horse is following and equidistant from this line on each side.

Riders, who are past masters in the art (if one can call it that) of twisting words, do not hesitate to say that a horse is or is not "straight on a curve." As awkward as this expression may seem, it simply means that the horse's spine is then adjusted very exactly to the curved line it follows and that its hind feet exactly follow in the tracks made by the forefeet.

Up to this point everything is still quite clear. When one says of a horse that it is "straight," one simply notes a clearly visible fact which anyone can verify.

But an important observation must immediately be added: This fact in no way corresponds to the natural behavior of the horse, mounted or unmounted.

A horse at liberty is only occasionally straight and most often momentarily, *just long enough to show that straightness is by no means impossible or even difficult for it.* Usually, apparently normally, its hindquarters deviate from the line followed by its shoulders, perhaps because it is looking toward the right or left and the resulting movement of the neck affects the hindquarters, which deviate in the opposite direction, or perhaps for some reason impossible to guess, sometimes perhaps merely an instinctive caprice. The same tendency may be seen in dogs.

And the same behavior is true of a mounted horse when the rider leaves it plenty of freedom of the neck and avoids any intervention with it. So if a mounted horse is and remains straight in its movements, *it can only be the result of schooling.*

We must then amend our definition of a straight horse: In equestrian language, the word "straight" not only expresses the *fact* that we have established, but also the *quality acquired* by the horse, thanks to which the rider can ensure and control its straightness easily and precisely.

Finally, one can attribute the quality of straightness to a horse only when its rider is always able to place it exactly, from head to hips, on the straight or curved line it is following, the coincidence of the tracks made by the forefeet and hind feet then being only the consequence of this placement and merely offering a means of verifying its precision.

Obviously the rider can place and maintain a horse "straight" only if he has the means to control its posture in the lateral sense, that is to say the means to act with sufficient effectiveness and precision on the position of the horse's head, neck, shoulders, and hips.

The schooling he must accomplish in order to have a straight horse thus consists of acquiring these essential means, which obviously involve achieving submission to the aids in this particular utilization.

We have seen that the control of *speed* as well as of the horse's *vertical position* (its posture observed in profile), and consequently of its *equilibrium*, depends on both hands acting simultaneously and equally, combined with the comparable action of both legs.

The precise control of the horse's *lateral position*, which leads to absolute control over its *direction*, can depend only on the action of one hand or the other and of one leg or the other, used separately or in combination. In short, the schooling required for obtaining straightness in a horse is thus quite simply schooling in obedience to the aids used separately. We must therefore consider successively the horse's schooling to the "single leg" and to the "single rein."

By acting with only one leg, the rider can displace the horse's haunches to the opposite side.

The first condition is to make the horse perceive a sensation clearly different from the one to which it has learned to respond with forward movement. This result will be obtained by acting with the leg clearly behind the usual place on the horse's flank.* The next goal is to ensure that this new sensation leads to the desired reaction. But if the sensation is strong enough to provoke some kind of reaction, the horse instinctively reacts *against* it, in this case by displacing its hindquarters toward the right if the right leg was acting, and vice versa. So the rider will have to form an association between the action of the leg and another action that instinctively provokes the desired result. The most common, because it is most simple and effective, consists of using the stick in a series of light taps on the thigh or on the haunch, which provokes the desired reaction instinctively enough for it to be rapidly learned by the classic procedure of punishment-reward-repetition. It is generally advisable to give

* Later, at a more refined level of equitation, this action can be made almost without any displacement of the rider's leg by exerting a pressure from front to back instead of perpendicularly.

this lesson on foot to start with. When it has been well learned, the mounted rider will be able to associate with the maximum effectiveness the action of his leg with the action of the stick, and thus obtain the desired response.*

In this case, just as in schooling to the action of both legs, a good quality of obedience will result from the observance of the same two principles:

1) The action should be interrupted, with the leg keeping a light contact in the same place, as soon as it has been obeyed, if necessary repeating it when it has been obeyed insufficiently or when it ceases to be obeyed.

2) If the obedience is insufficient, do not try to improve it by applying a stronger leg action, enforced by muscular strength or spurs, but on the contrary try to make the action more clearly understood and respected by returning to the means that renders it more explicit and can, if necessary, make it more re-spected—in other words, the stick.

It goes without saying that, to the extent that his horse obeys the action of one leg or the other, the rider will have provided himself with the means to modify and control the lateral posi-tion of the hindquarters.

The problem of a single hand action is exactly the same as that of the two hands acting simultaneously, which we have already studied in chapter 3. Again, it consists of substituting for the instinctive reaction of "counterreaction" provoked by the action of one hand, an acquired reaction of yielding. The procedures to use and the principles to observe in applying them are identical.

To the extent that his horse yields to the action of one hand or the other, the rider will have provided himself with the means of placing the horse's forehand in the lateral position he wishes and of getting the horse to assume and maintain this position without any resistance contractions; that is to say, without any muscular action other than what is naturally required in order to assume this position.

The absence of resistance to the action of one hand is obvi-

---

* This lesson of the single leg is described in every good book on riding, which is why I do not think it necessary to describe it in greater detail.

ously just as important as when it concerns the two hands employed simultaneously, and for the same reasons already given.

These, then, very succinctly summarized, are the special preliminary lessons the rider should undertake in order to provide himself with the means of placing his horse "straight." Of course, the result will depend not only on the quality of these means but also on the quality of their utilization. *Theoretically*, this may seem simple and easy. *Practically*, every rider of any experience knows that it is neither simple nor easy.

In fact, it is very difficult. And it is useful to ask why, in view of the principle whereby we must first recognize the nature of a difficulty in order to determine judiciously not only the procedures to utilize *but, above all, the intelligent way to apply them.*

Why, then, is it so difficult to place and keep a horse "straight"?

The traditional explanation is that the horse's body is naturally incurved laterally. Many people believe that this incurvation is innate and results from the position of the foal in its mother's womb, where it tends to be curved toward the left. Others believe that it is acquired and results from the fact that horses from their youngest age are always approached from the left and handled with the right hand, and this in time develops in them the habit of curving their bodies to the left rather than to the right.

But both of these explanations, which are in no way contradictory, can satisfy only those people (the majority, I believe) who maintain that almost all horses are incurved to the left. However, there are also horses incurved to the right, maybe a good number of them.

As an illustration of how much this question has always troubled horsemen, there is the following anecdote reported by General L'Hotte:

"Monsieur de Sainte-Reine, a fine horseman," claimed that horses were incurved to the left because they carry their manes on that side and that in order to straighten them one had only to make their manes fall to the right, for "in order to observe the movements of its rider which attract its attention to the right as well as to the left, the horse has to turn its head farther to the right than to the left due to the obstacle represented by the mane in its line of vision." And General L'Hotte gently adds, "Perhaps this is true of horses with very bushy manes, but not with the others, at least not that I have been able to observe."

Since then, there has been plenty of time to see that horses whose manes are clipped behave no differently from horses that wear their manes long, on one side or the other!

What should we think of all this? Quite simply, in my opinion, that this search for an explanation is only of very relative, not to say insignificant, interest, because *if one accepts the theory that horses are incurved*, it matters little whether it is manifested more often on one side or on the other. The problem of "straightening" them is exactly the same.

What matters more is to ask whether or not horses really are incurved. Strictly speaking, *they are not*. Incurvation is the state of what is and *remains* incurved. But no such thing is observable in any horse, either in the stable or at liberty—not even mounted, if it is reasonably free in its movements. Not even (which seems to me convincing) when it sleeps standing up, with its neck held low, always perfectly in line with the axis of its body.

This so-called "incurving" thus appears only when the rider adjusts and uses his aids. All one can say in this case is that the horse then assumes a posture that is more or less incurved on one side, or merely that it seems to be more natural and easier for it to incurve itself on that side. It would thus be only a habit, a tendency, or a greater facility for incurving itself on one side than on the other. One might then conclude that the initial cause could be a difference of lateral suppleness.

It is quite true that on horseback one often has the impression of a greater stiffness of the neck, even of the entire spine, on a certain side. How often, for example, it is said: "My horse is stiff on the right side." But has anyone ever seen the same horse show the slightest difficulty in snatching a lump of sugar that its rider holds out to it from the saddle in his right hand? And can you imagine the same horse, bitten in the right flank by a fly, being unable to scratch the spot with its teeth because it lacks suppleness on that side? Well, then?

Well, then, quite obviously, the impression of stiffness is not due to lack of suppleness. It is due to the fact that the existing suppleness is no longer manifested *because of contraction.* It is not at all involved with any physiological, muscular, or articular problem, which would require appropriate "gymnastics" based on "suppling exercises." Besides, the lateral incurvations of the neck and spine required in equitation, even in high-school dressage, are never very pronounced and thus never demand any extraordinary degree of suppleness. All horses without exception are supple enough to produce them—*on the sole condition that they are willing to do so.*

So in order to understand the difficulty of making a horse "straight," one must first exercise a little intellectual honesty and put aside, once and for all, the false reasons that riders are always prone to find for excusing their clumsiness or incapacity and for explaining their failures. We must therefore limit ourselves to what is undeniable.

It is undeniable that perfect symmetry does not exist in nature, no more in the animal kingdom than in the vegetable kingdom.

It is also undeniable that in the animal kingdom, a certain physical asymmetry, so slight as to be usually imperceptible, is always complemented by a distant asymmetry of behavior which seems to have no possible physiological explanation.

For example, there is no physiological reason for a person's being right-handed or left-handed, or much more rarely (and never perfectly) ambidextrous. An athlete in the high jump instinctively makes his take-off more naturally from one foot or the other, even if his musculature is very evenly developed. Ballet dancers undergo strenuous training in order to acquire the perfect symmetry of movement that is essential to their art, and yet they never succeed in performing the most difficult movements as easily and as brilliantly on one side as on the other—a fact that a choreographer always takes into account when composing a ballet for a particular dancing star.

We can then logically admit that this asymmetry of behavior is also true of animals, including horses. Some Thoroughbreds, for example, run better on a counterclockwise race course than on a clockwise one, without its seeming valid to blame this on any innate or acquired incurvation or on any difference of lateral suppleness, considering the very great range of turns they have to make. Some jumpers seem more at ease in approaching an obstacle on a left lead than on a right one, or vice versa. Couldn't they simply be more or less "right-handed" or "left-handed"?

If a creature already displays a certain asymmetry in its physical behavior when it is totally free in its movements and entirely left to its own devices, as in the case of man or of a horse at liberty, it seems reasonable to admit that when this behavior is submitted to external intervention, as in the case of a mounted horse, the asymmetry should be affected.

Even supposing, however, that the rider's position on horseback is always perfectly symmetrical (which is far from being the case), his actions never are, no more on horseback than on foot. Can any rider claim that he uses each of his legs and each of his hands equally, with the same skill and the same force? I doubt it. Furthermore, the rider is usually unconscious of his asymmetrical behavior, simply because it is instinctive and because he has never tried to be aware of it or to correct it. If the rider's actions are not symmetrical, how can he expect the horse's reactions to be so?

And since the instinctive reactions of the horse to the rider's actions are always characterized first of all by certain resistance contractions, isn't it logical to admit that it is perfectly natural for these contractions to manifest themselves asymmetrically?

The fact is that every horse has an instinctive tendency for a particular kind of asymmetry. If the rider pays no attention to it during the first schooling session (which is almost always the case), the horse settles down in this asymmetry. It organizes, in a way, "its own" asymmetrical form of resistance.

It is easy to see how this asymmetry can in time become a habit, all the more deeply rooted because, through ignorance or ineptitude, one or several riders will have neglected it and will even have contributed to reinforce it. It is consequently all the more difficult for another rider to correct it.

Need we probe the question further? I do not think so, because we would run the risk of getting bogged down in an endless discussion, impossible to conclude in a satisfactory way since it would concern cases that are individual to each horse, and to each rider as well.

We have nevertheless established:

• first, that certain difficulties encountered in seeking to obtain straightness originate in the horse, but that they may well be due much more to an asymmetrical behavior than to any physiological asymmetry, innate or acquired; and

• also, that the rider holds an equal share of responsibility, the importance of which is impossible to specify, but the existence of which is undeniable.

It must be admitted, however, that the ideal method whereby the cause is suppressed in order to dispel the effect is inapplicable here, partially at least. For if, theoretically, the rider can acquire symmetry in his actions through constant attention and hard work, he cannot make the horse different from what nature has made it, nor can he change the fact that its behavior tends to be first of all instinctive.

In the case of a mounted horse, this *instinctive* behavior is the result of two kinds of reactions: its reactions to the circumstances, which, as we have seen, constantly induce it to deviate from a straight position; and its neuromuscular reactions to the rider's actions.

Since it is unnatural for a horse to *remain* straight, its straightness must be acquired, or taught, and can only result from schooling, thanks to which its personal reactions will no longer be manifested and its reactions to the actions of the rider will be symmetrical.

Its personal reactions to the outside world and to circumstances will no longer be manifested if the rider can, thanks to a strictly enforced and totally accepted control, capture its attention so completely that the outside world no longer exists for it.

Its reactions to the rider's actions will be symmetrical if it yields with the same degree of submission to the actions of the right hand as to the left, and to the right leg as to the left.

Once stripped of its false elements, the problem of "a straight horse" is thus reduced to a simple problem of submission to the aids.

Since the rider's actions engender contractions which are manifested more on one side than on the other, due to the natural asymmetry of the horse's behavior, there is no point in trying stubbornly to "supple" that side more than the other, because its suppleness is not in question. What should be done is simply to eliminate the resistance contractions as much from one side as from the other, which naturally implies paying more attention to the more contracted side.

I know that there are trainers who more or less consciously proceed in quite the opposite way. When they notice a stronger resistance on the right rein than on the left, for example, they increase their resistance on the left by pulling on the left rein. They thus succeed in equalizing the horse's resistances and in re-establishing a certain symmetry of behavior. But you can see where that can lead—not very far, at any rate!

In a dressage performance, for example, a fairly skillful rider (and fairly strong, too, if need be) can thus "present" a horse that goes straight along the center line and stops straight at the letter X or G. But a competent judge will not assess the horse's straightness from these "performances," even if they are very good. He will judge it in the equal facility of the horse's incurvation during turns and voltes, the equal amplitude of its two-tracks and changes of lead, even in the regularity of its strides at the trot, during the passage or the piaffe, etc. In other words, he will judge it in everything that can enlighten him as to the symmetry of the horse's behavior resulting from its equal submission to the right and left aids of its rider.

It is only in order to furnish an example that I have referred to high-school dressage. The purpose of this study of the word "straight," like all the preceding ones, is to deal with a problem of ordinary riding and schooling; no more. But it brings up the following question, which some riders have undoubtedly already asked themselves in reading these lines: What is the true importance of straightness in equitation?

I think I have already suggested the reply in discussing the problems posed to human beings in their physical activities by their naturally asymmetrical behavior. For ballet dancers, to repeat, it is of the highest importance to achieve as far as possible a perfect symmetry. But for sportsmen it is not necessarily true. In soccer, for example, a player should certainly try to be as skillful and effective on one foot as on the other. In swimming or bicycle racing, and in certain athletic specialties, relative symmetry is necessary to the quality of the style and of the effectiveness resulting from it. And we have seen that riders would surely have great interest in paying attention to it too. But in certain other athletic or sporting disciplines, such as javelin throwing, tennis, or golf, this is not the case. Likewise, the importance of symmetry in a horse, that is, the importance of establishing its straightness, depends a great deal on the particular discipline in which it is used.

In high-school dressage it is essential. A perfect harmony of movement cannot exist without perfect symmetry of the horse's muscular play. Every contraction manifested asymmetrically is obviously injurious to this harmony, which is thus impossible to achieve without having previously eliminated the resistances.

But, in the other equestrian disciplines, it is essential only to varying degrees, which rapidly decrease along with the lesser levels of control and the lesser equality of submission required.

In jumping, for example, after a horse has cleared a water jump, it is certainly important that the rider take it in hand again to slow down straight, because any swinging of the haunches right or left could lead to a disengagement or disequilibrium liable to impair the quality of the next jump or the precision of a required turn. It is also important for a jumper to be able to turn almost as easily to the right as to the left, since its successful clearing of an obstacle coming out of a turn can depend on it, as can the tenths of a second saved which often decide a victory.

A good polo pony should be just as handy on one side as on

the other, or almost, since the effective shot of a ball or the speed of a decisive move can depend on it.

But for a cross-country horse or a racehorse, straightness is of only rather limited importance as long as the horse is controllable.

In short, the idea of straightness is of real value and interest only in high-school dressage, and the word "straight" should thus have a place only in the vocabulary of this particular discipline.

In the other fields of equitation, it is not at all necessary for a horse to be rigorously straight. It is sufficient for it to be symmetrical enough in its behavior to be practically as handy on one side as on the other. But, in one case as in the others, the problem to solve is still of the same nature. And it should be stressed one last time, since it concerns uprooting an idea as false as it is tenacious and, moreover, propounded by many of the most famous riding authorities, that this problem consists not in seeking to develop equal lateral suppleness in the horse on both sides, but in obtaining from it an equal submission to the right and left aids, equally free from contractions, thus permitting its natural suppleness to be manifested equally on both sides.

In conclusion, let us simply note this: Just as the horse's submission to the simultaneous actions of both hands and of both legs leads to what might be called longitudinal handiness, its submission to the independent actions of one hand or of one leg leads to what might be called its lateral handiness. Highly developed, it can lead to straightness, which finally expresses nothing but the perfection of this lateral handiness.

Riders have long felt the need for a word to express what they feel on the back of a horse that is perfectly handy in all directions. This word is "lightness," and it is the subject of the next chapter.

12. Lightness

"Lightness," literally speaking, is the quality of an object of little weight.

When one speaks of the lightness of a ballet dancer, for example, it means that the dancer hardly seems to weigh anything because he or she moves with ease, vivacity, suppleness, and grace, without giving any impression of effort.

The word "lightness" has been adopted into the equestrian language with very much the same meaning. A mounted horse gives the impression of lightness when it moves with ease, vivacity, suppleness, and grace, without giving any impression of effort. Since it is mounted, this implies that it is perfectly at ease underneath its rider, perfectly in harmony with him, and that the rider consequently does not encounter the slightest difficulty in making himself obeyed.

"It is then that, for the spectator, the horse would seem to move with the lightness of a bird," wrote General L'Hotte, who, by using the conditional, clearly expressed that it was a question for him of an ideal, almost of a dream.

It is very important to think for an instant about this interpretation of the equestrian meaning of the world "lightness"; in other words, about this conception of lightness.

Not only is lightness much more than, it is also something quite different from, the other elements, the other problems of riding, such as calmness, impulsion, equilibrium, and straightness. It is the supreme goal of equitation, which can be attained only when all of its constituent problems have been solved.

Lightness expresses an ideal, *the ideal of equitation*, what one might think of as its perfect goal, as a quality permitting the total satisfaction of the rider's aspirations.

To have an ideal! Some people, in equitation as in life, do not seem to feel the need for it, if one judges by their behavior on horseback (or in life)—a behavior that often seems to reveal only the more or less ambitious quest for results as tangible and immediate as possible, and by any kind of means. But to have an ambition without being guided toward its attainment by an ideal has never been a good rule either in equitation or in life.

Be that as it may, and whatever kind of equitation is practiced, the riding ideal is simple and obvious: to ride a calm horse from which one readily obtains perfect *obedience*—immediate, precise, and energetic—for the performance with the greatest *ease* and the greatest *generosity* of everything that may be asked of it.

Having defined this ideal that in riding language is called "lightness," let us now analyze it in order to see how it can be attained or at least approached.

The possibility of obtaining perfect *obedience* from the horse with the greatest facility depends quite simply on its perfect submission to the aids.

Assuming that this has been accomplished, the horse can evidently be at *ease* in its performance only if nothing disturbs it from beginning to end. Its ease thus depends on the physical and psychological comfort it is given.

The horse's physical comfort depends first of all on the quality of the rider's seat, thanks to which their two bodies can move in perfect harmony—one might say, like perfect dancing partners. But it also depends on the freedom the rider gives it during the performance by interrupting every demanding action as soon as it has been obeyed, while maintaining only the contacts necessary for producing a possible future intervention with precision and without surprise.

The horse's psychological comfort, which is expressed by calmness, results from the confidence its rider has succeeded in inspiring by the precision, clarity, and justice of his commands, that is to say, by the perfect use he makes of his aids.

The horse's *generosity* in its performance is nothing but the expression of its impulsion, the nature and means of development of which we have already studied in detail.

So it is finally quite clear that the word "lightness" simply defines the behavior of a horse that is perfectly submissive to perfectly applied aids; in other words, of a horse that is perfectly schooled and perfectly ridden. Simply that!

It is, in fact, so simple and obvious that it is almost embarrassing to use such ordinary words to express an idea that has been the subject of so much discussion and that remains controversial. Can I fairly be accused of possessing an outrageous spirit of oversimplification for having dismissed the problem without really having dealt with it?

I do not think so, and in order to prove it I shall once again call on the testimony of General L'Hotte. I have deliberately restrained my use of quotations during these studies, for my goal has been to invite the reader to join me in analyzing the problems of riding with a mind as free as possible from any previously acquired knowledge; in other words, from preconceived ideas. Since it does not express in any way a limited technical problem, as we have established, the word "lightness" can have only a conventional meaning. This is why, not presuming to innovate but only to clarify the question, I feel the need to seek support from L'Hotte, who, according to General Decarpentry, gave French equitation its "body of doctrine," and whose ideas, in France at least, are accepted without dispute (at least verbally or in writing, for actual practice is something else).

General L'Hotte devoted a chapter of his *Questions Équestres* to lightness, from which I extract only these three paragraphs:

"What it has been agreed to call lightness is the perfect obedience of the horse to the lightest indications of the hand and heels of its rider.

"Lightness thus characterizes at the same time the state of a horse that is perfectly well schooled, and the correctness of the means employed to direct it.

"It follows that the expression *lightness* is applied both to the horse's schooling and to the rider's talent."

Which is exactly what I have been saying.

Lightness is not at all a goal to be sought only at the end of schooling, as some people claim or teach, a final stage to cover after the other objectives—impulsion, equilibrium, engagement, and straightness—have been attained.

Lightness should be the ideal that is constantly pursued from the very start of a well-conceived and successfully accomplished schooling program. This should be obvious, since lightness expresses perfect obedience to the aids (please excuse me for harping on it), and every step of progress toward this obedience is a step toward this perfection.

As simple and as elementary as it may be, this conclusion is nevertheless of the greatest importance, for the entire conception of schooling, of its goal and of the means of attaining it, are thereby clarified.

Please remember, too, what we have already established:

• *Impulsion* essentially expresses the perfect obedience to the leg actions from a horse that not only does not fear the hand but is confident in it.

• *Equilibrium* cannot be controlled without perfect submission to the aids and particularly to the hand, since it is the hand above all that is able to adjust the position of the horse's "balancing pole" (its head and neck), which governs to a great degree its distribution of weight.

• *Engagement* is nothing more than the result and the physical expression of generous impulsion contained by a completely accepted hand.

● *Straightness* cannot be obtained or approached without a very high degree of obedience to the action of the aids employed singly.

● Even *calmness*, if it is not natural, can result only from a confident and absolute submission to the aids.

The development of these different qualities can therefore be crowned with success only to the extent of the progress that is achieved in submission to the aids. The perfection of each of them is simply inconceivable if the horse's submission to the aids is not perfect.

A horse that is perfectly calm, forward moving, straight, well balanced, etc., thereby shows proof of perfect obedience to the hand and to the legs, and it will therefore be *light*.

So it is by the degree of lightness attained that one can measure exactly and exclusively the quality of a horse's schooling.

Now is the time to pose the same question that we asked concerning straightness: Does lightness have equal interest and importance in all the equestrian disciplines?

It is clear that if lightness is considered as the achievement of a perfection, it can really be reached only in high-school dressage. We will return to this.

It is nevertheless true, and fortunately so, that high-school dressage specialists are very far from being the only ones capable of feeling the joy we mentioned at the beginning of this chapter—the joy of riding a horse so responsive that it is possible without effort to get it to obey instantly while displaying the greatest of ease and the most complete generosity.

But this joy is obviously available only to very good riders with horses whose schooling is perfectly adapted to their utilization (and this schooling may be quite elementary as long as it is sufficient for the utilization).

This can be the case of a jockey whose horse is calm at the start of a race, springs ahead at the starting signal in a supple and free action, can be placed easily wherever his jockey chooses in the field and at the speed that he decides, and responds to the first movement of his wrists either to furnish a momentary effort or to go all out when the time arrives for it.

It can be the case of a polo player whose pony is always high-spirited but with which he does as he wishes whenever he wishes so easily that he hardly has to think of it, and who thus is free to devote all his attention to the action of the game.

It can be the case of a show jumping rider whose horse is never lacking in generosity but permits him to control its speed and direction with ease, thus enabling him to ride with precision and without resistance and to adjust its equilibrium, engagement, and the placement of its take-off according to the problems encountered.

Is it possible to speak of lightness in regard to these horses? Can one say that they are "light"? The word is obviously not very appropriate. It somehow does not seem to go well with the athletic nature of the effort required by competitive equestrian sports, which can sometimes be terrifically intense, for example at the finish of a race or when clearing a huge jumping obstacle.

To offer a comparison, one can speak of lightness in regard to the leap, sometimes prodigious, made by a ballet dancer, but the word does not come to mind when speaking of an athlete who clears a height of six feet or more, however beautiful his style may be.

The word lightness is thus appropriate only in artistic equitation, and not in sporting equitation. There is no reason to be surprised by this, because those who chose it and defined it were thinking only of high-school dressage, which was the only equestrian discipline that existed at the time, as the sporting disciplines had not yet been created.

But if the word is not appropriate, the ideal that it expresses is perfectly valid.

This ideal, which the high-school experts call lightness (and which sporting riders might well agree to call something else), may then be "the perfect obedience of the horse to the actions of the hand and heels of its rider." General L'Hotte's definition remains valid by simply substituting the word "actions" for "the lightest indications." The meaning is in no way altered. Although in competitive riding sports there can be no question of "light indications," for they require clear and firm actions, these actions should never have to be violent and certainly not brutal, which would quite obviously imply either that the horse's obedience is very imperfect or that the rider rides very badly.

As further proof that the idea behind General L'Hotte's definition of lightness has equal interest and value for all equitation of high quality, let us quote him again. After briefly mentioning the consequences that inevitably result from the horse's resistance to the rider's actions or from the "lack of agreement between the rider and the horse," he adds: "Lightness . . . finds its formula in the rider's putting into play and the horse's utilization of only the forces useful to the desired movement."

Isn't this the ideal toward which every rider, sporting or not, should aim? Would anyone dare claim that there is no disadvantage in a horse's spending part of its muscular and nervous energy in resisting or defending itself against the actions of its rider? Well, that is what it is all about.

Whether a horse is jumping a big triple or performing a series of flying changes of lead at every stride, it is irrefutable that the application by the rider or the utilization by the horse of forces, in other words of muscular energy, that are of no use in clearing the first or in performing the second, can only be harmful not only to the horse's store of energy and generosity (which it is always condemnable to waste needlessly), but also to the style on which largely depends the effectiveness in the first case, and entirely depends the beauty in the second.

So, once lightness has been disencumbered of all the hazy or simply erroneous thinking to which it is so often subjected, we can conclude simply this:

● The word is appropriate only in high-school dressage, for which it was originally adopted.

● The idea it expresses is nevertheless valid for all equitation of high quality, for such equitation is inconceivable without a high level of schooling, inasmuch as perfection in the utilization of a horse, whatever the purpose may be, can be attained only to the degree that perfection in its schooling has been achieved.

13. To Observe, to Think, to Experiment

Before presenting a few photographs to illustrate a certain number of the ideas previously expressed and at the same time to suggest subjects for personal observation, I would like to propose one more morsel of food for thought.

Equitation is obviously a sport, inasmuch as, whether practiced for pleasure or in competition, it requires physical activity and effort.

It is also an art, in the primary sense of the term: "An ensemble of knowledge, of means, of procedures, and of rules of action which enable one to do something well." One can speak of the "equestrian art" just as well as of the "military art" or the "medical art."*

But equitation can also, to a certain degree, be considered a science—an experimental science, of course—and this merits closer examination. In the experimental sciences, the object of a study is submitted to an experiment, as is certainly the case in equitation, but on certain conditions. An experiment is scientific

* If the word "art" is used in its sense of "a means of expression of beauty," equitation may be considered an art only in its academic branch of high-school dressage, which can, to a certain extent, be compared to the art of dancing.

. only if its goal is to provoke an observation with the intention of studying or confirming certain phenomena and certain reactions, and also of verifying an idea or of drawing other ideas from the result. A method may be called experimental only if it consists of observation, then of a reasoned analysis of the results, leading to a hypothesis for research, and finally to verification by practical experiment. A method based solely on the elements furnished by a mechanical performance of certain practices is merely empirical.

Medicine used to be based principally on empiricism, until the great scientific discoveries of the eighteenth century; until then, it was very rudimentary and uncertain. Some doctors, of course, succeeded more or less in becoming "healers," but most of them, consciously or not, were hardly more than charlatans.

Equitation was empirical until the nineteenth century and has generally remained so since then, for the very few riding masters who tried to impose a reasoned equitation in place of an equitation that was simply instinctive attracted very few followers. This is why its progress has been so unsteady. Of course, there have been and always will be a certain number of highly talented riders. But, as noted before, how many true masters are there who have been capable not only of personally attaining the summit of their art, but also of aiding its progress by transmitting their knowledge and by teaching others who might eventually equal and perhaps surpass them? On the other hand, how many charlatans there have been!

The experimental science of equitation can be only partially learned from books. Books on equitation can, however, aid effectively by proposing subjects for observation and experimentation as well as guidelines for reflection and research. But it is then up to each rider to make his own discoveries through his own practical experience.

Throughout the preceding pages, I have therefore limited myself to logical deductions, based whenever possible on easily verifiable facts of observation. This is because I believe that as soon as a rider has acquired the essential technical bases for achieving freedom of body and mind, he should constantly *observe, reflect,* and *experiment.* The primary element of this triple process is observation. Guided and exploited by intelligence, it is observation that furnishes the material for reflection, the results of which will then be put to the test of experimentation.

In order for an observation to be valid and profitable, it must firstly and above all be objective, free from any preconceived ideas as to its results. This is obvious. The condition is quite easy to fulfill when observing a horse at liberty, and also (although a bit less so) when observing a horse mounted by somebody else. But when one is in the saddle oneself, observing the behavior of the horse one is riding, the situation is very different. In this case, the observation is always applied to the result of an experiment that is in the process of taking place. Observation and experimentation are thus simultaneous. Furthermore, in experimenting with one's horse, one is also and necessarily experimenting with oneself. In order to be valid, the rider's observation must therefore be applied not only to the behavior of his horse, but also to his own behavior, the first always depending on the second to a degree that it is impossible to determine exactly, but that is always very important. A supplementary difficulty should be noted: the rider's observation can be only partially visual. He should therefore acquire and develop other means of perception of a tactile nature, through his seat, hands, and legs, in order to "feel" what he cannot see.

It is logical that the rider should seek the origin of difficulties and faults as well as of successes and progress first of all in himself, and only afterward in the horse. Objectivity toward oneself is certainly not easy to achieve, or even to approach. But doesn't one of the keys to human behavior, as well as to equestrian behavior, consist of knowing how not to underestimate or overestimate oneself?

Now let's get on to the photographs. They certainly cannot replace real-life observation, but they can often guide or confirm the latter. And that is their only purpose.

The horse possesses beauty and harmony, power and agility, generosity and good nature. It is one masterpiece of creation that has ever had an extraordinary attraction for man. It is up to us, as riders, to enhance the value of this animal by developing and using these gifts, but above all to do everything possible to avoid degrading it. PHOTO BY WILLIAM C. BROOKS

These young horses still know man only through the care they have received from him. Full of health, they have already developed in their free gambols strong and harmonious musculature. On the alert, interrogative perhaps, a little anxious probably, they would be easy to startle, but they don't show the slightest sign of hostility. To deserve this wonderful gift of God, to succeed in being generously served by them and not merely to use them, the rider must acquire the necessary physical techniques, but he also has to employ all the qualities he has of sensibility, psychological understanding, and intelligence to make use of this technique to achieve complete success. That is equitation, much more and better than a sport. PHOTO COURTESY OF LARRY M. LANSBURGH

At liberty, any young horse shows the main qualities that one must aspire to rediscover in it when ridden. If the rider succeeds, without using constraint, to get its full and confident acceptance of his physical presence and of his moral authority, its generosity, its instinctive aptitude for carrying itself in the right balance, the harmony, the scope, and the energy of its gaits will manifest themselves again. It is the first goal of any schooling. In order to reach it, one has to provide the means of making oneself understood.
PHOTO COURTESY OF LARRY M. LANSBURGH

A horse at liberty can be schooled to understand the visual or aural sensations that its master makes it perceive. It is then obedient to voice and gesture. PHOTO BY PAUL DE CORDON

A mounted horse must be schooled to understand the tactile sensations that its rider makes it perceive by the actions of his hands and legs. It is then obedient to the aids. PHOTO BY PAUL DE CORDON

To bring schooling to its full conclusion, whatever its goal, the principal problem for the rider, certainly difficult but fascinating, is to win the horse's consent to action. Only then can the rider successfully ask the horse to furnish its best efforts, and aspire to the finest performances.

William Steinkraus (USA), Olympic individual Gold Medal winner in 1968, Silver Medal by team in 1960 and 1972, highest scorer in the Olympic Prize of Nations 1972. PHOTO BY JEAN BRIDEL, "L'ANNÉE HIPPIQUE"

But a horse has its own will, and its willpower is undeniable. Even the most authoritative and energetic rider has often had occasion to observe it in the form of vigorous opposition. And when a horse wants something, it is always capable of making the most extreme change of direction, speed, or balance. PHOTO BY O. CORNAZ, "L'AN-NÉE HIPPIQUE"

Good equitation begins when the wills of the man and of the horse are bent toward the same goal. Certain courses performed by great jumping riders certainly are fine illustrations of this.

Pierre Jonquères d'Oriola (France), Olympic individual Gold Medal winner in 1952 and 1964, Silver Medal by team in 1964 and 1968, World Champion in 1966. PHOTO BY O. CORNAZ, "L'ANNÉE HIP-PIQUE"

Whatever the equestrian discipline, it is the horse and only the horse that accomplishes the required performance. The role of the rider, *after having obtained obedience*, is to permit his horse to make the most of its means thanks to his unity with it and to the freedom he is able to give it during the performance.

Janou Lefèbvre (France), Silver Medal by team at the Olympic Games in 1964 and 1968, World Champion in 1970. PHOTO DELCOURT

The horse is alert, attentive, ready to obey: this is calmness.
Commandant Lesage (France), Olympic Gold Medal winner, in-
dividual and by team, in the Dressage Grand Prix, 1932. PHOTO BY
PHOTO BLANCHAUD, SAUMUR

Total generosity, great energy, but imperturbable calmness and submission: this is good impulsion.
Adjudant Patrick Le Rolland, of the Cadre Noir of Saumur (France), French Champion of Dressage. PHOTO DELCOURT

This fine all-around rider, Larry M. Lansburgh, has a deep and supple seat, and he does not bother his horse with any intervention by the aids. This well-schooled cutting horse knows what it has to do. In these conditions, and in spite of the weight of its rider, it controls its mass perfectly during the most abrupt changes of movements. It is proof of perfect equilibrium.

Concentrated on the play he has to make, this polo player, firmly seated in the saddle, has easily made himself understood by his pony. The pony knows perfectly how to stop in equilibrium and how to prepare to make a half turn in order to follow the ball.

PHOTO BY WILLIAM C. BROOKS

When it gives its all to its activity, every horse naturally engages itself in an extraordinary manner. These two colts have certainly never performed a shoulder-in, but they obviously never needed to be "taught" how to engage themselves. PHOTO BY PAUL DE CORDON

Engagement of the hind legs also permits the horse to hold itself back on a slope and to control its equilibrium. It is quite natural and instinctive. The rider has only to let it do so. PHOTO COURTESY OF LOS ALTOS HUNT

This horse undoubtedly felt that its young rider was leading it to the obstacle a bit too fast. It engaged itself strongly in order to slow down and to rebalance itself . . . and then it jumped nicely and in complete security. PHOTO DELCOURT

It is going to require an enormous effort to clear this big obstacle
attacked from quite a distance. Engagement resulting from a firmly
stimulated but exactly controlled impulsion has created the "spring-
ing possibility" necessary for its success.
Pierre Jonquères d'Oriola (France). PHOTO BY JEAN BRIDEL, "L'AN-
NÉE HIPPIQUE"

The preparation for the jump has been accomplished perfectly. The rider, now concerned only with not interfering with her horse during its great effort (7 feet) is in perfect unity with its movement and gives it complete freedom. Effectiveness is then expressed in harmony and beauty.

Kathy Kusner (USA), Olympic Silver Medal by team in 1972.

PHOTO BY O. CORNAZ, "L'ANNÉE HIPPIQUE"

In collection, the engagement of the hind legs is only one element of a general posture characterized by equilibrium more on the haunches and an elevated style of action. PHOTO COURTESY OF OF-FICE NATIONAL AUTRICHIEN DU TOURISME

This rider's aids are extremely discreet, because she does not need to apply the slightest force in order to maintain her horse at the "passage" in impulsion and complete submission. This is lightness. Helena Petushkova (USSR), World Champion of Dressage in 1970, Olympic individual Silver Medal in 1972, and, by team, Gold Medal in 1972 and Silver Medal in 1968. PHOTO BY O. CORNAZ, "L'AN-NÉE HIPPIQUE."

14. Equitation and Tradition

During a visit to the National School for Advanced Physical Education, Louis Leprince-Ringuet, of the Académie Française, stressed the need for "continual re-examination of acquired knowledge," meaning ideas and principles that previously have been accepted as fact. His words did not in the least shock his audience of sportsmen.

But could anyone believe that such a statement would receive the same reaction at Vienna or Saumur, or even in the upper spheres of equitation in general?

In equestrian matters, doesn't a "re-examination of acquired knowledge" run the risk of impairing sacred *tradition?* And isn't it also a sign of arrogance? We are learnedly told that there is nothing left to be discovered in equitation, since the Great Masters who are landmarks in its evolution found out everything, explained everything, and established forever the "immutable principles" to which we all ought henceforth to conform.

The problem is that the roster of Great Masters (and the list of Great Principles, for that matter) are not the same for everybody. And we can then quite rightly wonder just what "tradition" really means.

Is it not merely another one of those words that are used and abused and that cease to have true meaning? One of those words that, according to the people and the facts, become bloated and then degenerate, causing the gravest risk of alteration and decline to the ideas they express?

It is therefore essential first of all to define "tradition" exactly, before seeking what is or what should be behind it.

The great zoologist Konrad Lorenz wrote: "A culture is based on an equilibrum between two mechanisms: the acquisition of new information and the conservation of acquired knowledge. Both are necessary. *Tradition represents the mechanism for conserving knowledge.*"

He went on to say in substance that the development of a culture thus presupposes a balance between tradition and change, between conservatism and challenge. The maintenance of too rigid a tradition leads to sclerosis, even to degeneration, if the knowledge it is supposed to conserve, being disputable in whole or in part, is not worth conserving, at least in its current state.

In order to retain its meaning and value, and in order to remain really alive and beneficial, tradition should therefore maintain a bond between the past and the present, taking into account the constant evolution of circumstances. And this requires from those who are responsible for it a constant alertness and an objective, open mind in order first to perceive and analyze this evolution and then to examine to what extent the established knowledge is affected by it and may need to be modified or adapted.

Tradition does not simply have to be preserved, like the collections of a museum, which need only to be protected from the ravages of time. It must also be cultivated, rather like a piece of land, which must certainly be protected from erosion, but must also be continually worked in order to maintain its fertility and if possible to improve it.

If this conception is correct (and it seems to me incontestable), certain dangers immediately come to light. They are, of course, habit and routine, as well as conservatism and rigidity. All possess a common factor: intellectual laziness.

Tradition is also exposed to another danger, which, although of a different kind, is just as great: the danger of alteration, even of falsification in the worst cases. Due to its very nature, tradition cannot be formulated in a definite way. Its transmission, often by word of mouth, lays it open to great risks. Aside from any question of competence, knowledge, or good faith, it is only natural for those who are supposed to be responsible for it to stress some of its elements and to neglect others, depending on the education they have received and the use they make of it, as well as on each individual's personality.

This reminds me of a choice remark the fine musician Pierre Boulez recently made to a journalist: "Tradition? The word reminds me irresistibly of the parlor game in which a phrase is rapidly whispered by one player to another. You begin with 'The moon is shining through the pine trees,' and it ends up in the last player's ear as 'The cow ate a piece of chocolate.' Tradition is like that—the deformation of a message through countless links of a chain. There comes a time when you have to refer back to the original idea."

Tradition should thus be a living thing but undistorted. And this is as true for equestrian tradition as for all others. But is it the case? Unfortunately, not at all. The truth is that the word "tradition," having lost its true meaning in equestrian language, has become a catchall.

Perhaps it is convenient this way, because everybody can interpret it in his own way. But it thereby loses all the value of the strict concept it ought to express. This is why I would like to discuss tradition in equitation, for it is of great importance to the quality and progress of riding.

When one considers the subject in depth, one is obliged to admit that it has become so vague and confused that one may well wonder if it still exists. How could things have reached this point?

The answer, I believe, is quite simple. Equitation, like many other human activities in the domains of science, technology, and art, as well as of sport, has evolved more during the past one hundred years than during the previous centuries since it originated. But, during that same period of time, what could and should have been its tradition became congealed, and the bond it ought to have formed between the past and the present gradually became slack, if not completely broken.

Under such circumstances, and it is the saddest aspect of the matter, the traditionalists, consciously or not, became merely conservators. Under the pretext of preserving all the inheritance of an old past, they refused to reject its erroneous elements, to re-examine the debatable ones, to adapt to the new forms of equitation what was worth keeping. And of course they did not accept, unless very reluctantly, the "innovators," even if they brought very valuable information or concepts.

In order to reconstruct the facts, it would be necessary to show, through a historical and technical study, what happened in equitation in the main riding countries, especially in France and Germany, which were the leaders in this field until the beginning of this century. Such a study provides a great deal of teaching facts and good material for reflection. But it would take us quite far from the scope of this book, and I am not sure that many people are still interested in the history of equitation. So I think it more desirable to look at the present time, the product of this history after all, in order to see what are the predominant, most common ways in which modern riders are practicing equitation.

Of course the way of riding of a rider who has practiced a great deal reflects more or less his own physical and mental characteristics. And everybody can observe that very experienced riders often develop a very personal style and sometimes even a personal technique of equitation. I think, however, that any way of riding can be classified in one of the two following categories: empirical equitation or rational equitation.

Empirical equitation was the only one until the nineteenth century and still is widely prevalent. It can itself be divided into two subcategories: the purely instinctive and the mainly methodical.

In *"instinctive empirical equitation,"* the rider exerts himself to develop his instinct by riding as many different horses as possible, no matter what their schooling, so as to eventually acquire the correct reflex, the "sense" of effective action in order to counter the horse's resistances or defenses. The advantage of this concept is obviously its extreme simplicity and the easiness that results, since it reduces to an elementary minimum the schooling of the horse as well as the theoretical instruction of the rider. Of course this simplicity can be considered sufficient if the goals of the rider are themselves very simple, as is the case with pleasure riding. But if the goals are more ambitious, the disadvantages of the system immediately appear for both horse and rider.

Concerning the horse, this kind of equitation makes it work in a constant state of more or less intense, sometimes violent contraction. It therefore constantly expends an amount of energy notably in excess of what is actually required for the performance or movement in question. This is contrary to any sensible training methods, human or animal, in which the goal is to achieve the maximum result with the minimum expenditure of energy. It also obviously causes great wear and tear on the horse. And particularly with blooded horses, thus with the best, there is a strong risk that such physical wear and tear will be accompanied by a corresponding psychological wear and tear due to the constant excessive appeals to the horse's natural generosity, which then all too often turns into nervousness or violence.

Concerning riders, it is certain that the best can acquire through long and intensive practice a feeling for the horse's resistances and the effective instinctive reflexes of appropriate reaction. But all others, less gifted, are left with no other means of compensating for their inadequate feeling or imprecise reflexes than the use of force, which can lead only to a kind of riding that may sometimes be effective but that is inevitably crude and too often brutal. Besides, even with the best riders, the obedience obtained from the horse by such elementary procedures may be sufficient to reach a medium level, but it is notoriously insufficient for attaining the level of advanced equitation required for all the competitive riding sports and also, of course, for high-school dressage.

"Methodical empirical equitation" is characterized by the systematic use of processes and movements employed progressively from the easiest to the most difficult, the goal being to obtain from the horse total submission and complete handiness. Everybody knows that a great number of methods have been invented and progressively refined and sophisticated since the first were conceived in the Italian academies of equitation during the Renaissance period. Most of them now are ignored or more or less forgotten or abandoned. Today, the most famous is, uncontestably, the German method, its efficiency having been abundantly proved for a long time by the performances of the German jumping and dressage teams.* To understand the basic nature of the German method, one must know the concept of schooling on which it is established. By schooling, the Germans mean "the physical education of the horse by means of a gymnastic program related to a systematic progression." This quotation is from General Baron von Holzing-Berstedt (1867–1936), German equestrian authority who was president of the Fédération Équestre Internationale in 1935. The famous book by Gustav Steinbrecht, *Gymnasium of the Horse,* expounds this concept, and one can read therein this definition: ". . . the work of systematic mechanization and of gymnastic education of the young horse which we call schooling."

The weak point of this method is that, as a great number of experiences in many countries prove, it cannot be universally applied, because it requires from the riders as well as from the horses some particular aptitudes and a definite capacity for adaptation to it.

To succeed through this method, the riders have to be very patient, obstinate, and hard-working. They also need a great

* I purposely do not mention the also famous method of La Guérinière, which is still used by the Spanish Riding School of Vienna, for its goal is to perpetuate the style of high-school equitation considered classical in the eighteenth century, whereas the subject of this book is the equitation of today.

aptitude and, even more, a real taste for discipline. Not only do they have to be capable of strictly observing "the method," which needs a lot of self-discipline, but they also have to believe that imposing a strict discipline on the horse is the best if not the only way of breaking its instinctive reactions of resistance in order to acquire unconditional submission.

But not all riders have these abilities or this taste, and, among many others, the Latin people, for instance, are not very capable, to say the least, of acquiring them, even if they honestly try, as many of them unsuccessfully did.

As for the horses, the problem is about the same because, like humans, they do not all have the same "personality." The "systematic mechanization" which, if well done, can be accepted by some horses, could drive others mad or, at the opposite extreme, reduce to slavery and kill the souls of French Anglo-Arabs, of English or American Thoroughbreds, or, more generally speaking, of any hot-blooded horses.

Thus the German method, in spite of its great value, does not supply for a large majority of riders the answer to their search for improvement. Actually, no method can supply such an answer, because the results that can be expected from a method depend much less upon its value than upon the way it is applied. And this way itself mainly depends (leaving aside the question of personal ability or talent) on the understanding of the "why" and the "how" this or that has to be done or not done.

Only *"rational equitation"* tends to fulfill this condition, by providing the rider not only with processes grouped in a method, but also with a body of principles that enable him to employ them intelligently, thus more effectively.

The pioneer of rational equitation was François Baucher. His fundamental idea was that a rider could and therefore should understand the problems of equitation, which are obviously first of all problems of schooling, since the procedures for utilizing a horse necessarily depend on the procedures according to which the horse has been schooled.

This led him logically to trace back to the *causes* of difficulties encountered in order to try to correct them, in contrast to all his predecessors, who, without exception, had sought only to correct by empirical processes the *effects* they observed. The result of this research permitted Baucher to proclaim a certain number of "principles," which, for the first time, provided a basis for discussing not only equestrian method, but also equestrian *doctrine*.

For the first time, somebody told riders not only how but also why. For the first time, a Master succeeded in making his pupils understand and believe what he was telling them to do instead of being satisfied, as all his predecessors had been, merely to demonstrate his personal talent and to try to make them do as he did, with the results depending almost solely on the gifts and aptitudes of each individual rider. For the first time, too, and as a logical consequence, a horse's schooling could produce an absolutely unprecedented degree of submission.

Baucher's achievement was to wrest equitation away from empiricism, to set it on the path of common sense and logic, and, finally, to leave to posterity all the essential elements of a doctrine that is entirely valid for schooling and utilizing any horse for any purpose.

At first, his discoveries and his extraordinary performances in dressage (he was the first to accomplish flying changes of lead at every stride) raised a great wave of curiosity and interest. But in the end his conceptions did not prevail, partly because, in spite of priceless discoveries, his work was not completed. He was so conscious of this that he retained until his last breath that productive sense of dissatisfaction, so rare among horsemen, characteristic of all true scientists and great artists. But the main reason his work has not been kept alive is that it was violently attacked in the name of "tradition" by most of the "important people" of the equestrian middle, who were of course firmly conservative, in France and even more so in Germany. Thus "rational equitation" has never been adopted by any school or academy of riding in the hands of these "important people," and, if it has had followers, it has not spread beyond them.*

However, General L'Hotte, the best pupil of Baucher, who was not only a rider of great talent but also a man of clear and rigorous intelligence, worked and thought along the lines of his Master's principles. Knowing that riders always have a tendency to employ "procedures" without attempting to understand them, that is to say, by routine and instinct only, he refused to establish a "method." But he reached the summit of the philosophy of the equestrian art by establishing and formulating an ensemble of conceptions dealing with principles and support by reason, a view for the first time really meriting the term "doctrine."

His work is certainly the least disputable and the strongest base from which the methods of modern equitation should be re-examined. Throughout the pages of this book, I think that I have faithfully adhered to the fundamental ideas of his teaching.

In conclusion, I would simply like to add that my ambition has been to propose to the reader certain conceptions which, if he accepts them intellectually, will enable him to direct his personal work and to avoid being led astray into experiments with the countless procedures or instruments that man's ingenuity has empirically invented throughout the centuries and that still continue to be invented with no greater success.

I have also wished to expose a good number of false ideas of which the sole justification is "tradition" and which, like veritable taboos, have for so long blocked the progress of equitation by encouraging riders to employ false procedures.

Finally, I have tried to replace these false ideas with others based on common sense and logic, not as articles of faith to be accepted by habit or conformism, but as true, profound con-

---

* The reader surely understands that this classification of empirical equitation (instinctive or methodical) and rational equitation does not pretend to be rigorous. I know very well that, for instance, some riders being or pretending to be "methodical" or even "rational" often behave more or less instinctively when on the horse's back.

victions capable of enlightening riders and of guiding them in all their equestrian work and behavior.

I hope that the reader has not been disappointed by the absence from these pages of anything resembling a riding method or a schooling program, because I hope that I have succeeded in convincing him that a rider whose ambition is to practice equitation of quality must first use his brains correctly. Only then can he profitably and successfully undertake the personal discovery and intelligent experimentation of the practical means that must be brought into play on the physical plane.

After having personally tried several riding methods, and having observed a good many more in practice, I am certain that none of them is worthwhile if its application is not guided by an understanding as profound as possible of the rider's problems and of the means at his disposal. And it is simply to this understanding of equitation that I have wished to contribute.

The ways to obtain obedience from the horse by the action of the aids were discussed in chapters 3 and 6. Now, in the following pages, I will pursue a bit further the practical aspects involved in putting principles into action.

15. Principles
Put into Action

A Few General Ideas

Equitation can be practiced in many different ways, depending on whether the rider is interested in a simple outdoor leisure activity (hacking, trail riding, etc.), a sporting activity in one of the equestrian disciplines (jumping, Three-Day Event, racing, polo, etc.), or even an artistic activity (high-school dressage). But in whatever form it is practiced, the problems of the riders are much the same. They can thus be solved by the same means. Only the degree of quality with which they are solved varies according to the case.

The degree of quality required by one form of equitation or another depends on the difficulty of the activity for which the horse is to be used, and consequently on the preliminary schooling it should be given in order to perform its work in a satisfactory way.

For the rider, equitation—or the art of riding—consists of:

● 1) knowing how to remain on horseback in the most perfect possible conditions of security and comfort, and

● 2) knowing how to transmit his will to the horse and to make it accept it, that is, knowing how to make himself understood and obeyed in producing the required movements or performances.

For the horse, the rider is thus:

a) somebody who has to be carried, in other words a "passenger," and

b) somebody who has to be obeyed, in other words a "commander."

Consequently, the problems the rider has to solve fall into two distinct categories:

a) As a passenger, he should ensure his security and comfort in the saddle by appropriate gymnastic procedures, and at the same time reduce to the minimum the interference or discomfort his horse may feel as a result of his presence on its back. This is the purpose of learning to acquire a "good seat."

b) As a commander, he should learn to make himself understood in order to be in a position to demand obedience, then to exercise his command with intelligence, psychology, fairness, and authority. This is the purpose of learning to use the aids.

It is only logical that a rider cannot be a good commander if he must transmit his orders in conditions of insecurity and discomfort, which restrict his freedom of body and mind, and if he troubles his horse and prevents it from fully expressing its innate physical and psychological qualities in doing what it is asked to do.

These principles should always guide the rider in his work, since the quality of obedience and performance that he can and should aspire to obtain from his horse always depends on the quality of the command that he is capable of exercising.

●

In riding, one must never forget that it is always the horse that is the performer of the movements to be made and that furnishes the effort required to achieve the desired results.

In sporting equitation, for example, the horse is the "athlete" whose value depends

● 1) on its innate aptitudes, which in turn depend on its evolutionary, physiological, and psychological characteristics;

● 2) on its physical condition, which depends on the care it receives and on the training it is given;

● 3) on its schooling, which is a necessary preliminary to any utilization and which in turn conditions

a) the development of its innate aptitudes and of its physical condition, and

b) the exploitation of the possibilities thus developed.

The performances of a horse that has been properly prepared and schooled will then depend, within the limits of its ability, on the quality of the rider who utilizes it, or, more precisely, on the way in which its rider is capable of exploiting the horse's schooling in order to bring into play all of its natural ability.

The Rider's Seat

The purpose of acquiring a good seat is merely to solve the strictly physical problems of riding. It thus constitutes the gymnastic part of equitation.

The *seat* is the quality that assures the rider of his *security* on the horse's back and his *comfort* in the saddle at all gaits and in all circumstances, whatever the horse's reactions may be.

The seat depends on:

● *equilibrium*, which permits the rider to remain steady on the horse's back without the use of force, and

● *unity with the horse*, which permits him to follow the horse's movements closely and constantly, absorbing or diminishing its reactions by means of appropriate gymnastic procedures.

A good seat permits *fixity*—in other words, the absence of any involuntary or useless movement—and leads to *ease*, which is the result of security in comfort and creates the freedom of physical action essential to a correct and effective use of the aids, as well as the freedom of mind necessary to decide instantaneously and deliberately on the most effective actions to take.

Acquiring a good seat is thus of vital importance, not only for attaining one's particular goal, *but also because a rider who hasn't a good seat is a considerable handicap to his horse.* Feeling insecure in the saddle, he grips with his legs. Being uncomfortable, he becomes stiff and tires easily. Consequently, the horse constantly feels actions of the legs, hand, or seat that have no meaning for it and to which it can react only by contractions, defenses, or disordered movements. It then becomes even more troubled and more difficult to utilize. It is a vicious circle, which inevitably leads to riding that is incorrect, unattractive, and even potentially dangerous.

In order to acquire a good seat, the rider should

● 1) possess or acquire certain physical qualities, and

● 2) learn to exploit them by utilizing the appropriate techniques.

The physical qualities necessary for acquiring a good seat are:

● *Equilibrium:* The sense of balance is instinctive. Progressive practice is sufficient for adapting it to the particular problem of equitation, and the use of stirrups is an effective aid at the beginning. A rider's equilibrium is satisfactory only if it can be effortlessly maintained.

● *Suppleness:* This is the quality that permits the easy execution of movements of great amplitude. It depends essentially on the free play of the joints and of their ligaments as well as on the elasticity of the muscles involved.

● *Decontraction:* This is the quality of muscles whose "tone" (the state of partial and permanent contraction that governs the postures of the body, whatever its position) is reduced to a minimum. Decontraction can be manifested just as well in movement as at rest. In the first case, the movement is then free from any useless, parasitic contractions. Decontraction is thus a *passive phenomenon.*

● *Relaxation:* This is a *psychological state* that permits the rider to be conscious of a certain muscular region (shoulder, leg, etc.) and to ensure its decontraction. It is thus a *voluntary phenomenon.*

Relaxation permits *decontraction,* which is essential to the manifestation of *suppleness.*

It is important to realize that equitation does not, as is often falsely supposed,   require exceptional suppleness, since it does not involve movements of any extraordinary nature or degree. However, it is true, at least in the beginning, that most riders show some stiffness. But this stiffness generally originates not in any lack of natural suppleness, but in the instinctive contractions that appear as soon as they are on horseback, and that are due to apprehension or simply to the discomfort resulting from an uncertain equilibrium in the saddle and from the technical incapacity to absorb or diminish the shocks resulting from the horse's gaits. The real problem for the rider is thus not so much to become supple, but to become decontracted.

The effective gymnastic exercises are therefore basically exercises of relaxation performed on horseback, at a standstill, and especially in movement. They should consist mainly of movements designed to ensure the relaxation of the hips and legs, the shoulders and arms.

After these, certain other exercises may prove necessary, either in order to increase the rider's natural suppleness, in particular in the region of the lower back (these can also be practiced unmounted), or in order to correct certain personal defects of position or style.

But it is not enough simply to possess all the qualities enumerated above. The rider must also know how to utilize them:

● 1) in order to acquire and maintain effortlessly, thanks to a progressive muscular adaptation, the most favorable basic position, and

● 2) in order to effect with decontraction the movements necessary for maintaining his equilibrium and ensuring his unity with the horse.

The fact is that it is impossible to be in equilibrium on a moving object and to be constantly unified with its movement while remaining immobile in a given position, except in the very rare case when the movement of the object is perfectly uniform, as in an airplane that maintains the same speed, altitude, and direction.

Since the horse's movements are never uniform, even though they may be regular in their rhythm and scale, the rider can never ensure his equilibrium and his unity with the horse merely by assuming a fixed position, as appropriate as it may be.

The only way to solve the problem without the use of force—in other words, with suppleness—is to make certain movements that are exactly adapted to the horse's movements and are perfectly synchronized with them, while gradually developing good muscular co-ordination; that is to say, the ability to make the muscles concerned participate harmoniously in the execution of these movements, a condition not to be conceived of without a general state of decontraction.

ENSURING EQUILIBRIUM

The rider's equilibrium is constantly threatened, laterally by changes of direction, and longitudinally by changes of speed.

The movements that ward off these threats—for example, leaning toward the inside of turns—are simple and soon become instinctive.

This is valid, however, only when the changes of direction or speed are gradual enough so that it is possible to react in time. In the case of abrupt changes of direction or speed, more or less violent or unexpected, the rider would lose his equilibrium if it weren't for the adherence resulting from the weight of his body carried by his seat in the saddle, as well as from his legs enveloping the horse's body. Moreover, the less his torso is raised from the saddle, the more secure will be his equilibrium, which implies that the rider should stick as closely as possible to his horse, in other words, sit deep in the saddle.

It is important to note that the adherence of his seat and legs can be ensured only by starting from a judiciously adopted *position*.

Stirrups help greatly in maintaining the rider's equilibrium, or in re-establishing it when it is endangered, and their use is therefore recommended at the beginning. They can very soon be abandoned when working at a walk and a slow trot, in order to begin and to continue improving the achievement of unity with the horse, but at fast gaits they should be abandoned only gradually and in accordance with the progress realized.

ACQUIRING UNITY WITH THE HORSE

While the rider's equilibrium, reinforced if necessary by the adherence of his seat and legs, permits him to neutralize the effects of the horse's lateral or longitudinal reactions, it is of no use against the effects of its vertical reactions. Equilibrium alone cannot ensure the rider's *unity with the horse*, which is essential for a good seat. In order to acquire this unity, he must turn to gymnastic procedures similar to those used in solving similar problems by the circus rider who stands on the back of a galloping horse, by the skier, etc. (See Figures 1 and 2 on page 170.)

In fact, the only way to remain united with the horse in spite of its vertical movements (at the trot, the gallop, and when jumping) is for the rider to make appropriate and perfectly synchronized movements that neutralize the reactions he feels.

These movements may be divided into two categories according to whether the rider ensures his equilibrium by placing his weight in the saddle or on the stirrups. They can logically concern only the portion of the body situated above these support points, from which the reactions are felt.

● 1) Equilibrium in the saddle: The appropriate movements are made by the lower back, which means bringing the joints of the pelvis into play with the sacrum, the lumbar vertebrae, and the last dorsal vertebrae. (See Figure 3 on page 171.)

● 2) Equilibrium on the stirrups: The appropriate movements are made mostly by the legs, which means bringing into play the joints of the ankles, knees, and hips. When movements of very great degree are concerned, as in jumping, the entire body should participate. (See Figures 4 and 5 on page 172.)

Whether the movements are made by the back or the legs, the principle is the same: the joints involved should *close in order to evade* the upward push resulting from the rising movement of the horse's body, then *open in order to maintain contact* with the support points (saddle or stirrups) during the descending movement.

Of course, this evasion and this maintenance of contact can be ensured only to the extent of the possible degree of play of the joints involved; that is to say, their suppleness.

If the horse's reactions are of too great a degree to be totally absorbed in suppleness, or if they are too brusque (jumping, bucking, etc.), the most these movements can do is to diminish them, and they should be reinforced by the adherence resulting from the envelopment by the legs.

When the rider is seated in the saddle, the suppleness of his back, that is to say, the degree of movement of which his joints are capable, is limited. The horse's reactions can be absorbed only within the same limit. Generally speaking, the suppleness of the rider's back should enable him to absorb the reactions felt during medium gaits.

When the rider is on the stirrups, the degree of movement of which the joints of his legs are capable is naturally great. It can be utilized to the extent permitted by shortening the stirrups. He can resort to enveloping the horse's body with his legs when the degree of the horse's movement is greater than that of the movements of the legs permitted by shortening the stirrups, for example in jumping.

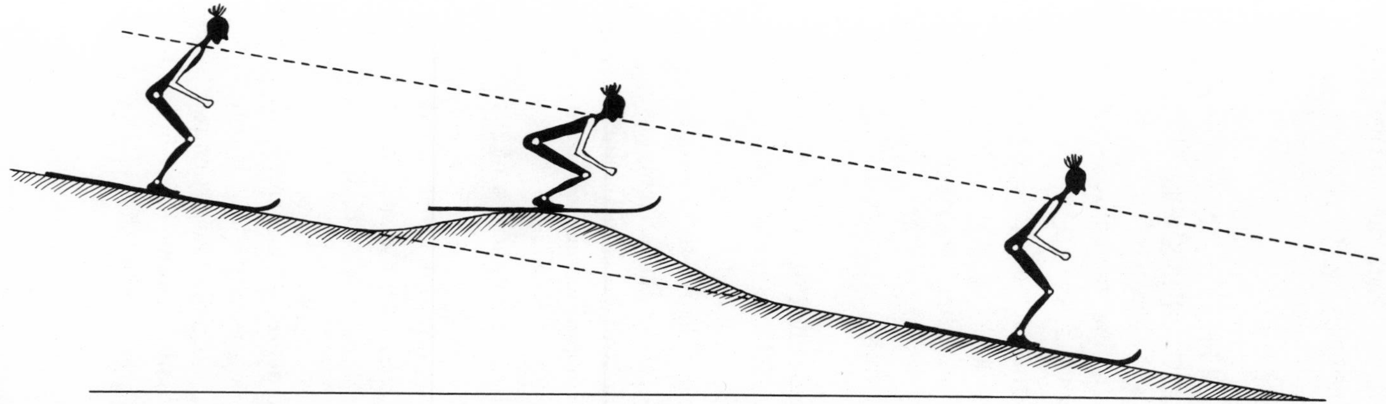

Figure 1

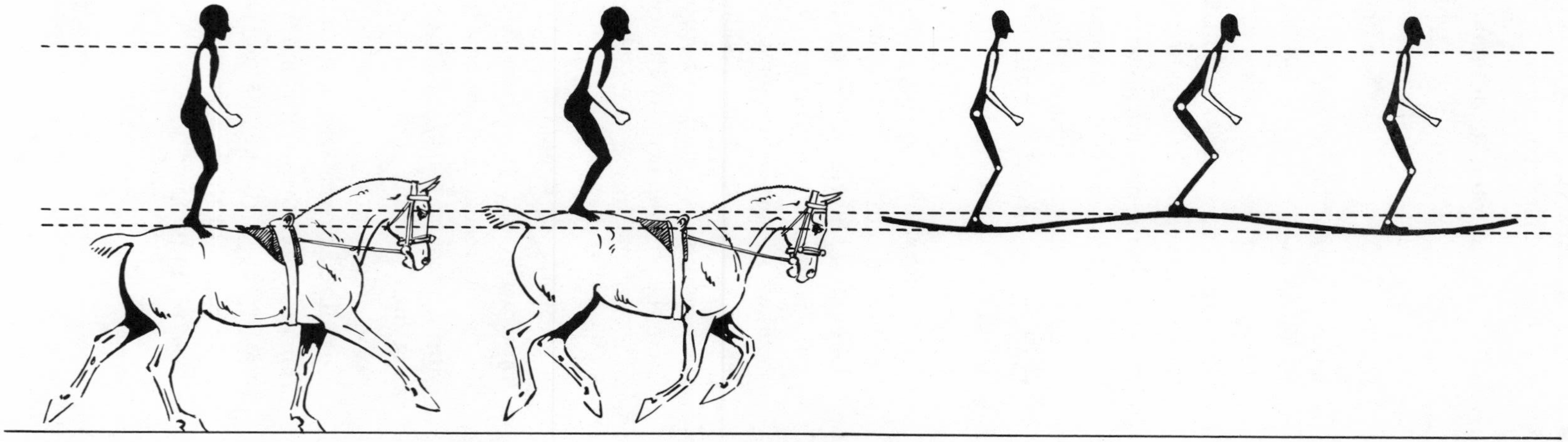

Figure 2

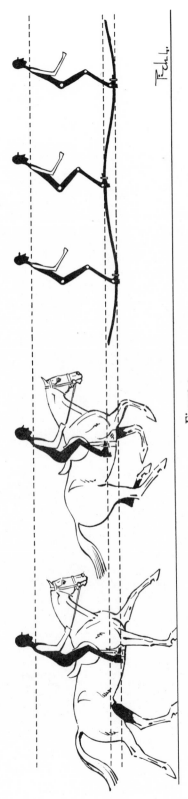

Figure 3

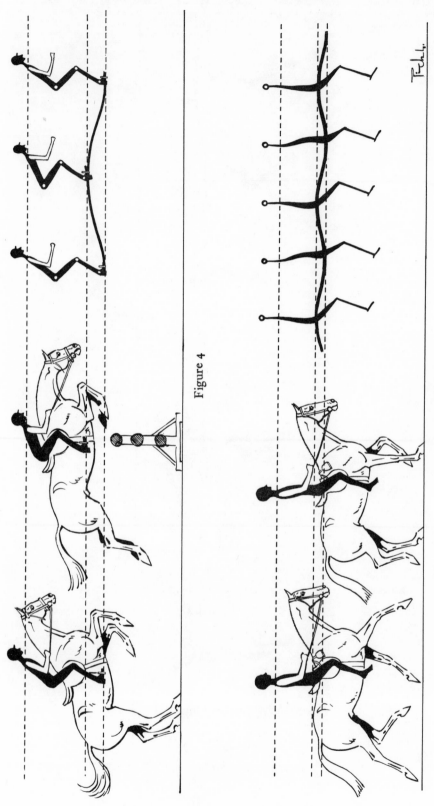

Figure 4

Figure 5

In order to complete our analysis of the seat problem posed by the necessity of absorbing or diminishing the effect of the horse's vertical movements, it should be added that when the upward push occurs, the inertia of the rider's mass tends to maintain his body at the same height. The rider should exploit this physical fact at the moment that he "yields" by closing the joints situated above the point where the push is exerted (the back when he is seated, the legs when he is on the stirrups).

He can thus seek the impression (which can be really true only when the degree of the horse's vertical movements is less than or equal to that of the play of his joints) of maintaining his shoulders on a more or less horizontal line while the horse rises and descends beneath him. (See Figures 1 to 5.) *He thus exploits his inertia instead of being handicapped by it.*

In any case, the rider's *position* is the rational and functional base from which the movements can be made most naturally, most easily, and most effectively.

The first condition of a good seat is thus a correct position, since it is absolutely necessary for ensuring equilibrium and for acquiring unity with the horse.

THE RIDER'S POSITION

The rider's position on horseback should fulfill three conditions:

● It should be as natural as possible, so that the muscles can easily adapt themselves to it and it can thus be assumed without contraction and held for a long time without fatigue.

● It should be functional; in other words, provide a technically satisfactory base for establishing a good seat and for performing the various movements required by equitation.

● It should be capable of reducing to the minimum the disturbance of the horse caused by the presence of a rider on its back.

In equitation, as in many other sports, striving for what is natural and functional leads to effectiveness in simplicity and finally to beauty.

The position described and analyzed below has become classic precisely because it satisfies these conditions and permits these results. As it is the most natural and most functional one, it is also the most harmonious and provides the best base for an effective but pure and elegant style, which should be the ideal of every rider.

- 1) *Position of the seat*

The rider should sit as far forward in the saddle as possible, on the fatty part of his buttocks, with his weight evenly distributed.

This position of the buttocks is the most important point, since it determines the position of the legs and torso. It thus conditions the execution of all the movements that ensure the rider's seat as well as his use of the aids.

The position of the buttocks concerns not only *where* the rider sits, but also *how* he should be seated.

a) *Where to sit*

He should sit as far forward as possible, close to the pommel, which corresponds to the region of the horse's back immediately behind the withers. This is the most favorable place for the horse as well as for the rider.

It is most favorable for the horse because its dorsal vertebrae situated there are almost fused together, so this portion of its back is practically rigid and originates no movement of its own. It can thus support the rider's weight without any local muscular contraction, consequently without any functional disturbance. On the other hand, the farther back the rider sits in the saddle, the more his weight affects the last dorsal vertebrae and the first lumbar vertebrae (which are progressively more mobile) and the more he interferes with their freedom of action, which is essential to the horse's locomotion.

Furthermore, when the rider is seated well forward, his legs are naturally placed on the first sternal ribs, the respiratory movements of which are so slight that they are no more bothered by the rider's legs than they are by the girth, which is also placed there.

It is also most favorable for the rider, because it is the most comfortable place for him to sit. First of all, it does not originate any movements of its own; second, the first sternal ribs, on which his legs fall quite naturally, are the flattest and most ogival in shape of the horse's entire rib cage, and are thus the least constrictive for the opening of the rider's thighs.

b) *How to be seated*

The rider should sit in such a way that his weight on the saddle rests not exclusively on the bony excrescences of the ischia (seat bones) but also partly on the fatty part of the buttocks. By pushing his buttocks underneath him in a forward direction, as if he wished to support himself on the sacrum, he will give his *pelvis* the proper position.

This position of the pelvis is essential. In fact, if the rider is seated only on his ischia, his pelvis, sacrum, and lumbar vertebrae are then placed on a line perpendicular to the horse's back, and the articulations involved transmit all of its reactions. On the other hand, if he is seated on the fat of his buttocks, his pelvis is inclined toward the rear, the articulations of the lower part of the back are already slightly flexed, and they are thus favorably disposed to yield to the reactions felt, as it is necessary for them to do in order to establish unity with the horse.

● 2) *Position of the legs*

The lower limbs should be allowed to hang freely, simply by relaxing the articulations of the hips, knees, and ankles.

● The thighs are then well descended without being tight, the knees are in contact, naturally (thus slightly) flexed;

● The legs fall freely along the horse's ribs;

● The toes, naturally low without stirrups but higher than the heels when the stirrups support the weight of the legs, naturally turn outward at the same angle as the thighs in relation to the axis of the horse's body.

This position is absolutely natural and results simply from the complete relaxation of the joints. It therefore can and should be obtained by a perfect muscular decontraction.

Except in very exceptional cases, the opening of the thighs that it implies remains within the limit permitted by the rider's natural suppleness. It thus requires no effort. Nevertheless, with beginners it generally causes soreness, for two reasons:

● first and foremost, because the instinctive tendency of the rider to ensure his security in the saddle is to tighten his thighs, and he thus brings into play muscles that are normally not very developed as they are seldom used.

● next, to a lesser degree, because the prolonged maintenance of this position, even without effort, is unhabitual and the muscles must adapt themselves to it progressively.

Soreness can thus largely be avoided by relaxing the hips, which permits all of the weight of the body to rest on the buttocks without tightening the thighs (except when necessary, and then only briefly and as little as possible).

● 3) *Position of the upper part of the body*

the back should be supported,

the torso at ease and erect,

the chest slightly thrown out,

the shoulders sloping and completely relaxed,

the arms falling vertically and the elbows thus remaining close to the body,

the forearms pointing toward the horse's mouth,

the wrists in the same line as the forearms,

the hands slightly separated, with the thumbs on top,

the neck erect and free,

the head straight, the nape of the neck far enough back, and the eyes looking high

This position of the upper part of the body is also very natural and can thus be maintained without useless contraction. However, it implies assuming a certain posture of the torso, and it thus excludes the total relaxation of the spinal articulations, for this would lead to its collapse.

The key to this posture is support from the lower part of the back, that is to say, maintaining the back in a position halfway between extreme flexion and extension. From this position, the back can act in both ways to the extent permitted by its suppleness, and can thus fully play its role in ensuring the rider's unity with the horse.

The relaxation of the shoulders, however, should be just as total as the relaxation of the hips, the first permitting fixity and independence of the hands, and the second permitting fixity and independence of the legs.

In short, the ultimate goals to aim at in acquiring a good seat should be:

● 1) to acquire the *position* corresponding to the physical conditions most favorable for solving the problems of equilibrium and of unity with the horse in a state of decontraction;

● 2) to acquire a sense of *equilibrium* on horseback, which is instinctive and thus only has to be developed and adapted by practice;

● 3) to acquire *unity with the horse* by learning to make the appropriate movements with suppleness, voluntarily and consciously at first, then, thanks to practice, more and more instinctively and unconsciously;

● 4) due to the progress realized in these first three points, to use the maximum adherence resulting from the multiplication and constancy of the points of contact (buttocks and legs), this adherence being necessary in situations in which the rider's equilibrium and unity with the horse cannot be completely ensured by means of suppleness alone.

To the extent that these goals are attained, the rider, having ensured his *security* and *comfort* in the saddle, at the same time avoiding any cause of useless hindrance or disturbance to his horse, will have acquired a *seat* permitting him to obtain the *fixity* and *ease* without which he could not possibly employ his aids correctly, precisely, and effectively.

The Aids and Their Use

The only means man has for communicating his will to an animal and obtaining obedience from it is to make it perceive physical sensations, which may be aural or visual if the animal is commanded by voice or gesture, but which are above all tactile in the case of a mounted horse.

The goal of schooling a horse, which is a necessary preliminary to any utilization, is to teach it to respond with appropriate reactions to certain tactile sensations that its rider imposes.

The rider who uses the horse afterward therefore has to learn to exploit the results of the schooling that his horse has previously received.

When a rider makes his horse perceive a sensation, he is said to be "acting on the horse." His action expresses his will to obtain some particular reaction, that is to say, a particular movement.

When a horse responds to the rider's action (in other words, to the sensation it perceives) by the desired reaction (in other words, by performing the desired movement), one can say that it understands and obeys.

In order for its obedience to be satisfactory, the horse's reactions must be immediate and generous, free from nervousness or violence.

The quality of the horse's obedience depends on the quality of the training it has received, but also on the quality of the rider who utilizes it; in other words, on the manner in which the rider is able to act on the horse. A rider who does not succeed or who succeeds only badly in making himself obeyed should therefore not place the blame on the quality of the horse's schooling before having made certain of the quality of his own actions.

The means by which the rider can act on his horse are called "the aids."

They consist of the "principal aids," which are the most effective and the most employed means of action, and the "complementary aids," which can be associated with the principal aids in order to facilitate or to improve their effectiveness.

The principal aids are the legs and the hands.

The complementary aids are the rider's weight, his voice, clucking of the tongue, the stick, etc.

We will limit ourselves here to a few generalities concerning the principal aids, in order to help the rider form a clear idea of their effect and also of the most effective manner of employing them.

In order to use these principal aids intelligently, the rider should never forget the following:

• 1) The horse's reactions to his leg or hand actions are learned through schooling. The more closely the rider's actions conform to those that the horse has been schooled to obey, the better will be the horse's reactions to them.

• 2) The actions of the hands or legs should never be thought of as a form of physical constraint obliging the horse to obey by force. The force they may require in case of insufficient obedience or, even more, in case of refusing to obey, can only have as an effect, and thus should only have as a goal, to make the horse feel the sensations strongly enough to overcome its laziness, inattention, or even unwillingness. The use of force in employing the aids is thus a means for the rider to impose his will by dominating the will of his horse, and the idea that he could dominate the horse by physical constraint is only an illusion.

In short, the rider should know that a horse can fail to obey, or can obey badly, for one or several of the following reasons: ignorance, inattention, laziness, unwillingness.

A horse's ignorance is due to the schooling it has received and thus does not concern us at the moment.

Inattention, laziness, or unwillingness can and should be overcome by the rider. Besides, they generally result from the ineptness or ineffectiveness of his own actions, which are either incorrect and therefore misunderstood, or timid and lacking in authority and therefore not respected.

The rider can use his principal aids in the best of conditions only when he has previously established good contacts between his hands and the horse's mouth through the intermediary of the reins and bit, and between his legs (more precisely, his calves) and the horse's flanks.

The quality of these contacts depends on their *constancy* and their *intensity*.

The constancy of the contacts should be absolute. Otherwise the rider's actions would have two serious defects:

 a) They would surprise the horse, which could lead to reactions that are sudden, more or less abrupt, even disordered; and

 b) they would be more or less irregular and imprecise, and thus could only lead to reactions equally irregular and imprecise.

The intensity of the contacts, manifested by the tension of the reins and by the pressure of the calves, should be as slight as possible as long as it is sufficient to ensure their constancy.

Contacts established with too much force necessarily lead to two serious inconveniences:

 a) For the horse, they represent a hindrance, even unjustified pain, and for the rider a useless effort, thus unnecessary fatigue.

 b) By creating sensations without significance, to which the horse becomes accustomed, they finally damage its sensitivity and consequently lessen the quality of its obedience to the rider's aids.

When the contacts established are good, that is to say constant and as light as possible, the aids are said to be "adjusted."

It is most important to realize that only the quality of the rider's seat permits him to have well-adjusted aids, because only a good seat can ensure the fixity and the independence of the hands and legs which are obviously essential.

In order to be effective, the hand and leg actions should fulfill the following conditions:

a) They should be *clear*, that is to say neither hesitant nor timid, so as to be clearly perceived by the horse.

b) They should be *exact*, that is to say they should be the same as those that the horse has been schooled to obey.

c) They should be *authoritative*, with just sufficient force to make the horse recognize the rider's determination to be obeyed.

d) They should *cease* as soon as obedience has been obtained, with the hands or legs resuming the simple contact necessary for possible subsequent actions.

Interrupting a commanding action as soon as it has been obeyed fulfills two equally important goals:

• It is the best way to make the horse understand that it has done what it was asked to do, and at the same time to reward it instantaneously with the immediate relief it feels from the interruption of the action.

• It is the only way to preserve the horse's sensitivity to the rider's actions, for to prolong them needlessly would only make it gradually become accustomed to them and react less and less. As the rider would then have to become increasingly insistent, the horse would become increasingly insensitive. It is a vicious circle, which should by all means be avoided.

To summarize, the rider should realize from the outset that his effectiveness depends on the progress he makes in the following endeavors:

• technically, the adjustment of his aids and the correctness of their actions, thanks to the quality of his seat;

- psychologically, his authority expressed with the necessary firmness and energy, excluding, of course, the slightest trace of brutality or anger, which are never justified in the exercise of any command.

Use of the Aids in Schooling

When a rider has acquired a pretty good seat and has learned how to use his aids fairly correctly and effectively with horses that are sufficiently calm and obedient, thus sufficiently schooled, he must realize that from then on, whatever the horse he rides, every act of utilization is also inevitably an act of schooling (see chapter 1, page 10).*

He should therefore think of himself not only as a utilizer who tries to get the best out of a particular horse by applying his aids according to the previously described rules, but also as a trainer, since he should try to get the horse to obey him more and more easily and better and better.

This concept is all the more necessary because from then on he will probably be riding horses that have already been given schooling that is either insufficient (as may be normal with young horses), or bad (as is unfortunately the most frequent case), or else inadequate for the proposed utilization.

So as soon as he is capable of riding a horse in a consistent manner with the intention of utilizing it for a particular purpose, every rider finds himself in the role of a trainer, since he should at least continue the horse's schooling, often correct it, and in any case improve and adapt it.

Disregarding or rejecting this concept amounts to blindly following the course of simple instinctive utilization by means of force and constraint; in other words, bad riding. Although this instinctive utilization can undoubtedly be somewhat effective and therefore satisfying at first, I have already sufficiently

---

* This is certainly not to say that the rider should be satisfied with only an approximately good seat and mastery of the aids. On the contrary, the progress he can hope to make as a trainer and utilizer depends on the progress he continues to make in these two respects.

pointed out its limited horizons as well as the risk of physical and moral destruction of the horse that is submitted to it.

Furthermore, as soon as a rider is responsible for a horse, he should also devote great care and attention to getting it and keeping it in the best possible condition.

He cannot logically realize his ambition as a utilizer, which is his ultimate goal, unless he has been able to provide himself with the necessary means by getting his horse in condition physically through care and training, and psychologically (calmness, submission, generosity, etc.) through schooling.

The question of physical conditioning is not within the scope of this book.

As far as schooling is concerned, I shall only state or recall a few principles which, if they are accepted wholeheartedly, will enable the rider to make a wise choice from among the numerous schooling procedures that are well known (or easy to learn from books), and above all to put them into practice most effectively.

CALMNESS ABOVE ALL

In all schooling, whatever its goal, an absolute priority should be given to calmness—to its constant maintenance when it already exists, and to its complete re-establishment if it happens to be lost (see chapter 5).

PROGRESSING VERY GRADUALLY

One of the best ways to guarantee rapid and successful results in schooling is to observe an extremely gradual progression when making greater or new demands of the horse.

Whenever he asks his horse to do something, the rider should, of course, have a clear idea of what he hopes to obtain, in other words of his ideal goal. But he should know how to be satisfied with the slightest progress toward this goal and to reward it. He should compare the result obtained not with the ideal goal, but with the result that was obtained the previous time, and he should be satisfied if it is just a little bit better.

This rule of gradual progress also obviously implies proceeding without haste from what is easy and well mastered to what is slightly more difficult and mastered less well or as yet not at all. It also implies, in the case of unusual difficulty in responding to some new demand, interpreting this difficulty as a sign that the demand was premature because the means available were insufficient for expressing it, for making it understood and obeyed. In such a case, the rider's immediate obligation is to improve the effectiveness of these means, which are the aids.

MAKING ONESELF ACCEPTED, UNDERSTOOD, AND RESPECTED

Schooling a horse is no more than making it accept, understand, and respect the aids.

In schooling to the legs (see chapter 6), the trainer should never forget that once the leg lesson has been well taught and understood, the principal obstacle to a frank and generous response by forward movement or acceleration lies in an insufficient acceptance of the hand and its actions. The rider should therefore take great care to precede all his leg actions by reducing the tension of the reins to the minimum required in order to maintain contact with the horse's mouth. Until the horse's submission to the hand actions is sufficient, he should also refrain, when he has obtained the desired acceleration and at the moment of slowing down, from making any demand that exceeds the means available for obeying it. A demand to slow down that requires considerable use of force because of insufficient schooling constitutes a veritable punishment for the horse, which will automatically associate it with the acceleration that it produced beforehand. Consequently, at the beginning of schooling (when fast gaits should be avoided anyway), decreases of speed should always be very progressive and obtained with a minimum use of force. Using the voice as an aid is particularly recommended in this instance.

In schooling to the hand, which is much more difficult, the absolute principle is that the rider should start by placing himself and his horse in the most favorable and easiest conditions for it. These conditions really exist only in slow gaits: the walk and the slow trot.

The rider should try to make his horse discover how it should react to the actions of the hand, according to the method previously described (see chapter 3, pages 47 ff.),* by working first at a slow—even a very slow—walk.

At a slow walk, the rider has no problem of seat or direction and can thus dispose freely and fully of his hands in order to devote himself to this delicate work with total concentration and tact.

For the horse, the slow walk offers several important advantages. First of all, it is very favorable to calmness and to a certain general relaxation, since it requires no muscular effort. Moreover, the neck and head movements characteristic of the gait are very slight, which makes everything easier for the horse as well as for the rider. Finally, experience proves that this unaccustomed gait makes the horse attentive without any use of force, because very light leg actions are sufficient to avoid an excessive decrease of speed or a halt, while the hand actions, strictly adjusted to the horse's reactions, never need to be as intense as they almost always must be at the start of fast gaits.

When the rider has obtained a satisfactory result at a slow walk, he can then test it very progressively, first at a faster walk, then at a slow trot, then decreasing from a slow trot to a walk, then going into a faster trot, then slowing down from the faster trot to a slow trot and to a walk and so forth. It is useful to demand halts only when the decreases of gait are quite good, and it is easy to obtain backing only when the horse performs a halt without any contraction of its neck or jaws and is thus in the condition required for responding to the hand action requesting it to step backward.

Here, too, in fact especially, the promptness and quality of the results are guaranteed by scrupulously gradual progress.

The rider should realize clearly that it is the *manner* in which the horse obeys that must be taken into consideration before

---

* Each of these lessons should be short but may be repeated many times after a moment of rest or relaxation.

passing on to the following stage, and not merely the fact that it obeys. The proper manner, remember, is characterized by the fact that the horse responds to the hand actions by yielding; that is, without reacting against them by contracting its poll and mouth. A decrease of speed can thus be considered satisfactory only if the horse obeys the hand action while maintaining its poll supple and lightly flexing it, without trying to evade the action either upward or downward. And it is obviously contrary to common sense to try to obtain such a result from a fast gait if it cannot be obtained when going from an ordinary walk into a slow walk.

Finally, it is most important that in this work the rider's one and only goal should be schooling to the hands. The acceleration of a gait (or the transition to a faster gait) can and should be very gradual at first, since its goal is not to obtain or to improve the quality of the horse's obedience to the legs, but only to verify that it can be effected without altering the previously established contact between the rider's hands and the horse's mouth.

So, despite appearances, this work, which can be performed on straight lines or on wide curves, is not yet the true work of extending and decreasing gaits, in which clear-cut and energetic transitions must be sought. But it is the indispensable preliminary.

THE HORSE'S MOVEMENTS ARE TESTS OF SCHOOLING

The horse's movements, whatever they may be, should not be considered goals in themselves. They are first of all and above all a means of testing the horse's submission to the aids. They can then enable the rider to perfect and refine this submission.

This is true of extending or slowing down the gaits as mentioned above, as well as of all the movements on one or two tracks, on a straight line, or on a circle, that have been invented and standardized throughout the ages.

A movement that can be obtained only by the constraint of forceful actions by the hands and legs not only accomplishes nothing, but is even usually harmful, for it leads the horse to resist these actions in one way or another and to harden itself to them.

So if the rider notices, for example, that he cannot obtain a shoulder-in without the use of force, he should conclude that the horse is not yet ready to perform the movement. He should therefore return to schooling to the aids and, in this particular case, to schooling to the action of one hand or the other as well as one leg or the other acting singly (see chapter 11, pages 110 ff.).

Failure to observe this principle inevitably leads to a kind of mechanization of the horse by constraint and routine, and sometimes even to stultification. It can produce only limited and mediocre results.

When, on the contrary, thanks to the horse's submission to the aids, the rider is in a position to demand a certain movement, he can then utilize the movement in order to improve and refine the horse's submission. Whenever he demands a certain movement, he should therefore try to obtain it by using less and less pronounced actions, the governing principle always being to try to obtain the same results with lesser actions. He is then in a position to obtain better results by doing just a little more.

ALWAYS ACT WITHIN YOUR MEANS

At the beginning of a schooling program and for as long as the results are not good enough to permit progressing to lively gaits in favorable conditions, the horse must still be physically conditioned, and this involves exercise in energetic, thus relatively fast, gaits. There must therefore be quite a clear distinction between schooling and conditioning.

At the start of schooling, the lessons in the aids should be short, but they may be repeated several times to good advantage (for example, two or three lessons of seven or ten minutes during a one-hour schooling period). The rest of the time can be devoted to developing the horse's muscles and wind, interrupted by short rest periods, without any other concern for schooling aside from seeing that the horse remains calm and active in the selected gaits. Should problems arise, the absolute principle is for the rider to adjust his demands strictly to the means he has of obtaining them without a struggle (that is to say, to adjust them to the degree of schooling attained), and whenever his means are insufficient for imposing his will, then any compromise solution is acceptable.

With very young horses, as well as with horses that are hot or difficult, work on the longe is particularly recommended for giving sufficient exercise without the risk of having to use the aids, especially the aids of the hands, in a violent manner. When it is feasible, it is also excellent to exercise the horse at liberty.

SCHOOLING JUMPERS

Schooling a jumper presents no special problem, since its goal is exactly the same as that of schooling any horse: to obtain submission to the aids corresponding to the desired utilization. It should therefore be accomplished according to the same principles.

Jumping an obstacle, like any other movement, should be regarded basically as a test of obedience to the aids. If this obedience proves to be insufficient, it should be improved by work on the flat.

The special work designed to develop or improve a horse's jumping style and, more generally, its jumping ability, can be undertaken to advantage only when its schooling is sufficient. Consequently, this work should not be considered a form of schooling in itself, but a sort of special gymnastic training that can be undertaken and accomplished successfully thanks to previous sound schooling.

THE RIDER ALONE IS RESPONSIBLE

Any kind of power involves the obligation to assume all of its responsibilities. Riders do not escape this rule.

The horse can never and in no way be considered responsible for the difficulties that inevitably complicate its schooling. The rider should always seek the causes of these difficulties in his own imperfections in one or more of the following three points: his seat, the bad or inadequate use he makes of his aids, and the gradual progression of the schooling program he has followed.

It is by himself progressing that a rider can make his horse progress. The horse's progress (within its individual limitations, of course) will thus depend upon the rider's. And the finest riders have always admitted that in equitation there is always something more to learn.

The Role of the Lower Back

Everyone agrees on the capital importance in good riding of the role allotted to the rider's lower back. Everyone also agrees that this role is a dual one, for it influences both the quality of the rider's seat and the effectiveness of his actions for producing impulsion.

However, due to the prevalence of certain false ideas on the subject, it seems to me worthwhile to analyze just why and how the muscles of the lumbar region can ensure this double function, once more respecting the principle that a preliminary understanding of a problem, even a strictly physical one such as this, is a condition or at least an aid to its sound solution.

As far as the seat is concerned, we have already described the lower-back movements that the rider should make in order to ensure the proper unity between his own mass and that of the horse in action. There is no need to repeat them here, but surprise and dismay are provoked by the fact that they are so seldom taught.

Some instructors think they are giving their pupils the key to the problem by telling them that their lower back should act like a spring. However, despite a certain semblance, this comparison is completely false. After having been distorted, a spring reacts with a force equal to the force that distorted it, resuming exactly its original form. The lower back obviously does not possess this characteristic of elasticity, nor does any other part of the human body, for that matter. The lower back is composed of the pelvic bones, the lumbar vertebrae, and the first dorsal vertebrae, all of which constitute its inert framework, and they are cased in a complex of muscles and tendons that ensure the maintenance of this framework in a given form, or its adjustment; in other words, its movement.

Of course, the muscles and tendons possess an elasticity of their own, which ensures the supple maintenance of the body's equilibrium and positions, as well as the support of its weight. This elasticity contributes to the adjustment of the permanent and unconscious state of demicontraction that is called "muscle tone." But it is extremely limited, and quite insufficient in the case that concerns us here.

The muscles do, however, have the ability to contract, and their contractions, which alone are capable of producing movements of the degree required in this case, depend on the cerebrospinal nervous system, which in turn is governed by the rider's will.

When the rider's lower back seems to be acting automatically like a spring, the fact is that the rider causes it to make movements of flexion and straightening, which we have already mentioned as being necessary for establishing unity with the horse.

Establishing unity with the horse therefore means deliberately effecting the movements that are exactly complementary to those of the horse. Technically, it is very much like ballroom dancing, at least in dances in which the girl is supposed to follow closely the lead of her partner. A good dancer who is relaxed, and thus perfectly supple, performs steps and movements that are exactly complementary to those of her partner, in the exact rhythm of the music, taking care not to overdo it (horrors!); in other words, not to do more than he does. She thus establishes unity—not with her partner, which would tend to make her cling to him tensely (horrors again), but unity with his steps, his movements; in short, with his dancing. She is then light in his arms. She is a good dancer.

A good rider should behave with his horse in a very similar way. He should perform movements that are perfectly complementary to those he feels from his partner-horse, and in exactly the same rhythm, taking care not to overdo it, which would be useless, unattractive, and even troublesome to his partner. He thus does not establish unity with the horse's body (which would tend to make him tighten his legs by muscular contractions, and this, inevitably spreading to the lumbar region, would reduce its suppleness); he establishes unity with the horse's movements, in this case with the movements of its back that result from its gaits. The rider thus must employ a veritable ballroom-dancing technique which might be called "the dance of the lower back," with the same requirements of active suppleness, rhythm, and harmony.

Isn't it rather surprising that this "dance of the lower back," as essential as it is to the establishment of unity, without which a good seat is impossible, is not the object of any systematic instruction?

Instead of that, what do we see in almost every riding school? Beginners, obviously more or less severely shaken up as soon as the horse goes into a trot, instinctively tighten their legs in order to stay on, which is quite natural. As a result, they more or less contract the back, with which nobody has told them what to do anyway. They thus absorb all the shocks, and only the force they apply in enveloping the horse's body with their legs prevents them from being thrown too high out of the saddle. Then, in the best of cases and by means of more or less inappropriate exercises, they are persuaded to yield to these shocks, to become "supple," as it is erroneously expressed. But they are not told that they must untighten their thighs, nor how they should try to bring the lower back into play. So, still in the best of cases, the shocks became soft instead of being sharp, which is obviously an improvement. But there are still shocks, and consequently no unity with the horse.

Afterward, it is every man for himself, for the role of the instructor generally stops at this point in regard to this particular subject. Some young riders (only a few, as it is easy to see) instinctively discover for themselves the "trick" that enables them to avoid this disagreeable, tiring, and useless bouncing up and down. The rest find their personal solution in resignation, habit, hardening, and in the development of their thigh muscles in order to give them "gripping power," as they used to say. In the long run, and at the price of soreness and even abrasions, they can become firm in the saddle. But a good seat, supple and united, which is necessary for the practice of a good quality of equitation, will always remain a mystery to them.

In good-quality equitation, it is not only a matter of being firm in the saddle, but of being in the saddle in such a way that it is possible to apply the aids with all the independence, precision, firmness, and eventually finesse that permit the exercise of a good command over the horse. And since the secret of this way resides essentially in the unity of the rider's seat with the horse's movements, it is logical to conclude that the lower back also plays a complementary role of great importance in the quality, thus in the effectiveness, of the rider's aids.

When it concerns the use of the hands, this is all rather apparent. But when it concerns the use of the legs, it is necessary to study the question in greater detail, because of the widespread theory that the action of the lower back can create an effect of impulsion.

It is not actually a "theory," to tell the truth, but merely the affirmation of an empirical opinion that is particularly popular with the followers of the German school but that has never been justified, to my knowledge, by any analytical theory. It is categorically asserted that the rider can push his horse forward by rounding his lower back, and this movement is compared to that made by a child in order to set a swing in motion, then to maintain or intensify its motion. The rider is advised to round his lower back while trying to "push" forward, or to "weigh" with all his weight downward and forward.

However, while how to make this movement is often quite well explained, as far as I know no one ever explains how it could have an impulsive effect.

Many riders therefore try to use the lower back in order to push the horse forward, with an obstinacy that is quite admirable, since this practice is rather tiring and leads to results that are generally poor and sometimes null, as is always the risk when one does not understand the "why" of what one does. So let us try to discover the true facts by analyzing the different elements of the problem.

First of all, the comparison with the use of the lower back on a swing is quite false, despite a certain similarity of movement. The fact is that the child can set his swing in motion only by utilizing his *inertia*, which he can do only by giving his mass a suitable movement thanks to a "back push," which must be rather brusque in order to be effective. If he did no more than round his lower back gently by tilting his pelvis, as the rider is asked to do, the swing would remain perfectly immobile.

Furthermore, the force of inertia that is put into play by his back push engenders motion only because it is applied to an extremely mobile object (the swing), and all the more so because the mass of this object is less than his own. In just the same way, when one is seated in a rather lightweight chair equipped with rollers and placed on a smooth surface, one can make it move forward by "back pushes."

Need it be repeated that the rider on horseback has nothing in common with such cases? First, because it has never been recommended that the rider give brusque back pushes, and also because, even if he did so, the force of inertia that he would bring into play would have only an imperceptible effect on the horse's mass, which is considerably greater than his own and extremely stable.

Now let's see if the rider can push his horse forward by rounding his lower back. Obviously not, for the simple reason that a push can be affected on a body only from some independent support point, which is evidently not the case of the rider on his horse.

Can he "weigh with all his weight" downward and forward? Again, no. His weight is what it is. Only his inertia would be of any possible use, but then he would have first to raise his body from the saddle and then let it fall back downward and forward. Nobody, needless to say, has ever advocated this form of action.

So what remains of these assertions in the form of theories? Not much. Once more, as so often in equitation, the Masters have been satisfied to express by more or less vivid formulas the impressions they have felt on horseback, and to describe, with the aid of more or less well-chosen comparisons or examples, the behavior that has obtained good results for them. But they have not been interested, or at least not enough, in analyzing their impressions and their behavior in order to understand them and then to be able to make them understood by others and to transmit them effectively.

Nevertheless, every rider of any experience knows that there is some truth in this business of "pushing with the lower back" or of "weighing down with the buttocks." What can it be?

It is quite true that with a *well-trained* horse a rider whose legs are well adjusted can, by rounding his lower back, provoke or stimulate forward movement, on condition of course that he opens his fingers at the same time.

But it is just as true that with a horse that is only slightly or badly trained, a simultaneous leg action is necessary. This is easily verified by the fact that when the rider moves his legs away from the horse's sides, the effect of his back action alone is absolutely zero.

It is therefore logical to deduce from this experience and observation that the horse's reaction to the action of the rider's lower back is not the result of any direct effect of the rider's body on the horse's body, but simply the result of special schooling, which, like all schooling, is necessarily based on an association of sensations.

Let's take as a starting point the basic truth that, in order for the horse to react to an action, whatever it may be, the action must make it perceive a sensation.

The first question to be answered is, then, the following: What sensation can the rounding of the lower back make the horse perceive? It can be no more than the sensation of a slight displacement of the rider's weight toward the rear. The horse feels neither a push nor a weighing down (false impressions, as we have seen). It merely feels the rider's weight no longer concentrated more or less over the seat bones, as is the case when he is sitting straight in the saddle, but definitely farther back, over the fatty part of the buttocks or even over the sacrum, depending on whether the rider tilts his pelvis more or less by more or less rounding his lower back.

This new sensation thus results only from a progressive change in the continuous and customary contact of the rider's mass. It is therefore certainly not a strong sensation, in fact probably very gentle. Still, due to the horse's great sensitivity, it is certainly perceived with a clarity that depends only on the clarity of the action that produced it.

However, there is still no reason for it to cause the slightest instinctive reaction. In fact, it does not cause any, as anyone can verify. If the horse reacts, it must therefore be a "learned reaction." And since the desired learned reaction in the present case is forward movement, it is quite obvious that the sensation caused by the rider's rounding his lower back must be associated with the sensation of pressure by the legs, to which the horse has already learned to react by obediently producing forward movement.

In fact, this is what happens—at least with riders who are instinctively gifted and capable of good muscular co-ordination thanks to a general state of relaxation. They are told to "weigh" with all their weight in the saddle. So they loosen their thighs and their entire weight rests on their buttocks. They are told to "push" downward and forward with their back. So they round their lower back and instinctively seek a support point in order to make a push. This support point can only be found on the horse itself, and the push can only be made from the calves, adjusted underneath the horizontal diameter of the horse's body, by closing the knee joints. The action is all the easier and more effective, since the entire body weight is resting on the saddle and the leg muscles are perfectly free to effect it.

So it is not a "push" that they make the horse perceive, but a "pressure" caused by squeezing, in a way, the horse's body between their calves and their buttocks.

The horse thus perceives the following succession of sensations: first, the one resulting from the rider's simply rounding his lower back as we have described, immediately followed by the sensations resulting from the simultaneous increased pressure of the buttocks on the saddle and the calves on the horse's ribs. It is obviously this last sensation, previously known and understood through schooling to the legs, that provokes forward movement—if, of course, the rider's hand does not oppose it.

From then on, everything becomes clear. As this special schooling is assimilated and refined, the pressure of the calves and of the buttocks, which is essential at the beginning in order to obtain or to accelerate forward movement, can be progressively reduced, since the sensation caused by the rounding of the lower back, which precedes it very slightly and in a way announces it, will be so closely associated with it that the horse will understand what it is going to be asked to do and will not even wait for the command that was necessary in the beginning—or at least the command can be reduced to a simple touch of the calves without any accompanying increased pressure of the buttocks.

With a very well-trained horse, the rider will thus have at his disposal a new impulsive aid, the effectiveness of which will depend entirely on the reflex character of the obedience that he has been able to obtain. And this new aid has the immense advantage of being readily accepted, since the use of force is excluded by simple impossibility, and it therefore causes no constraint and provokes neither disturbance nor correlative contractions elsewhere.

It should be added that in the case of sporting equitation, in jumping for example, the problem is exactly the same, on condition that the horse has received the necessary schooling. As long as the rider is in a position of suspension on the stirrups, his weight is perceived by the horse at the height of the stirrup straps. But as soon as he needs to make an impulsive action, on approaching an obstacle, for example, he must sit down with his lower back more or less rounded, so that his weight then rests in the saddle and his legs are thus completely free to act effectively. However, in doing so, he *first* makes the horse perceive the sensation of his weight in the saddle, which is very clear to it because it is quite different from the preceding sensation. And to a well-schooled horse this sensation distinctly says: "Watch out! He's going to use his legs. Let's go!"

We can now summarize the role the rider's lower back should play in good riding, and which it is not very difficult to make it play when one understands just why and how it can and should be used.

● 1) The rider's lower back enables him to acquire a seat that is united with the horse. Its movements of flexion and straightening, produced from the position of the pelvis that has been described, are the only means of ensuring this unity, without which effective aid actions are impossible—and without which, in particular, if all of the rider's weight is not resting in the saddle, there can be no completely effective action of the legs.

● 2) The rider's lower back can act as an impulsive aid: when the horse feels that it is being increasingly rounded, the lower back can, through the association of sensations that have been described, indicate, complete, and reinforce if necessary the effect of the leg action. In advanced equitation, and particularly in academic equitation, it can even replace the leg action almost entirely, with the accompanying advantages that we have mentioned.

Finally, we should not overlook a supplementary and very important advantage of this manner of using the lower back, which benefits the horse this time and is therefore also in the interest of the rider: not only does it eliminate the shocks resulting from a lack of unity, which inevitably provoke contractions in the horse's dorsal region, but it is a gentle action in the exact rhythm of the horse's movements and in harmony with the play of its back muscles, which thus remain, without interference, quite free to fulfill their vitally important role in the horse's locomotion.

So let's hope that one day the riders who take such pains to use their back muscles, believing that they are "pushing" or "weighing," will realize that they have been mistaken or misguided and have thus been expending their strength and energy in vain. Let's hope they will then discover that, on the contrary, by putting their lower back into play in suppleness and in rhythm in order to "dance well" with the horse, they create the most favorable conditions for using their aids effectively and at the same time place the horse in the most favorable condition for obeying them.